MENTAL HEALTH

A HOLISTIC APPROACH TO WELL-BEING AND SELF-CARE

Ethan Clarke

TABLE OF CONTENTS

SUMMARY

"Mental Health: A Holistic Approach to Wellbeing and Self-Care" is a book that looks at different aspects of mental health. Chapter 1 provides an introduction to the topic, including a definition of mental health and a consideration of the factors that influence it. The link between physical and mental health is also being investigated.

Chapter 2 is dedicated to understanding mental disorders. Different types of mental disorders are explained, their causes are examined, and the symptoms and diagnostic procedures are discussed. In addition, various treatment options for mental disorders are presented.

Chapter 3 focuses on stress management and emotional well-being. It explains what stress is and how it affects mental health. Stress management techniques are presented and the importance of emotional well-being is explained. In addition, the influence of stress on emotional well-being is considered and the role of mindfulness in stress management is discussed.

The book "Mental Health: A Holistic Approach to Wellbeing and Self-Care" provides a comprehensive overview of various aspects of mental health. It covers topics such as mental disorders, stress management, self-care, relationships, exercise and nutrition, and relaxation techniques. It is designed for readers who want to broaden their understanding of mental health and are looking for practical tips on how to promote their own well-being.

INTRODUCTION TO MENTAL HEALTH

WHAT IS MENTAL HEALTH?

Mental health refers to the state of well-being and stability of the mind. It includes the ability to deal with life's challenges, build positive relationships, regulate emotions appropriately, and live a fulfilling life. Mental health is an important part of overall well-being and plays a crucial role in personal happiness and quality of life.

Mental health is not only the absence of mental disorders, but also includes the ability to manage stress, maintain positive relationships, practice self-care, and find a balance between work and play. It's about accepting yourself, acknowledging your own strengths and weaknesses, and developing positive self-esteem.

People with good mental health are able to regulate their emotions, cope with stress, and adapt to change. They have healthy self-esteem and are able to build and maintain positive relationships. They also have the ability to recognize their own needs and provide for themselves adequately.

Mental health is a dynamic condition that can change throughout life. It can be influenced by various factors, including genetic predisposition, environmental factors, life experiences, and individual coping strategies. It's important to note that mental health isn't static and that each person has different needs and challenges.

Promoting mental health is of great importance as it has a positive impact on all aspects of life. People with good mental health tend to be more productive, have better relationships, are physically healthier, and have higher life satisfaction. It is therefore important to take care of one's mental health and take steps to maintain and improve it.

In the next sections, we will take a closer look at the factors that influence mental health, as well as the relationship between physical and mental health. We will also explore the different types of mental disorders and how they can be diagnosed and treated. In addition, we will look at stress management, self-care, relationships, exercise and nutrition, relaxation techniques, and prevention and long-term mental health.

Mental health is an important issue that affects us all. By addressing this issue and taking steps to boost our mental health, we can live a full and happy life.

THE IMPORTANCE OF MENTAL HEALTH

Mental health is an essential part of our well-being and quality of life. It encompasses the state of our emotional, mental and social well-being. Good mental health allows us to deal with life's challenges, build positive relationships, achieve our goals, and live a fulfilling life.

THE EFFECTS OF MENTAL HEALTH

Mental health has a significant impact on all aspects of our lives. It affects the way we think, our emotions, our behavior, and our relationships with other people. When we are mentally healthy, we are able to manage stress, adapt, and connect with others. We have positive self-esteem and can recognize and meet our own needs.

On the other hand, poor mental health can lead to various problems. People who suffer from mental disorders may find it difficult to cope with everyday life, build relationships, and achieve their goals. You may suffer from anxiety, depression, addiction problems, and other mental illnesses. The effects of poor mental health can also show up on a physical level, weakening the immune system and increasing the risk of physical illness.

THE IMPORTANCE OF PREVENTION

Promoting mental health and preventing mental disorders are crucial. By taking care of our mental health early on, we can reduce the risk of mental illness and live healthy lives. Prevention includes measures such as building resilience, managing stress, fostering healthy relationships, and creating a supportive social environment.

It is important to understand that mental health is not just the absence of mental disorders, but a state of well-being in which we can develop our abilities and reach our full potential. By taking care of our mental health, we can live a full and happy life.

THE ROLE OF SOCIETY

Promoting mental health requires a holistic approach that takes into account the individual, social and societal aspects. Society plays an important role in supporting the mental health of its members. It's important for society to create a supportive environment where people can talk openly about their mental health without being stigmatized.

Educating and sensitizing society about mental health is crucial. It is important to break down prejudices and misconceptions and help people recognize the signs of mental disorders and respond appropriately. Providing resources and support to people with mental illness is also important to help them access treatment and support.

In addition, governments and organizations should take steps to promote mental health in all areas of life. This may include the provision of mental health care, the integration of mental health into schools and workplaces, and the creation of mental health programs.

Overall, mental health is of great importance for our well-being and quality of life. By taking care of our mental health, we can live a full and happy life. It is important that we as individuals and as a society take action to promote mental health and prevent mental disorders.

FACTORS AFFECTING MENTAL HEALTH

Mental health is influenced by a variety of factors. It is a complex mix of biological, psychological, social, and environmental factors that all work together to determine a person's well-being. In this section, we will look at some of the most important factors that influence mental health.

BIOLOGICAL FACTORS

Biological factors play a crucial role in mental health. A person's genetic predisposition can increase the risk of certain mental disorders. Studies have shown that certain genes can be linked to conditions such as depression, anxiety disorders, and schizophrenia. In addition, neurochemical imbalances in the brain can also lead to psychological problems. For example, a lack of certain neurotransmitters, such as serotonin or dopamine, can lead to mood disorders.

PSYCHOLOGICAL FACTORS

Psychological factors also play an important role in mental health. The way a person thinks, feels, and deals with stress can affect their mental health. Negative thought patterns, such as constant rumination or pessimistic thinking, can increase the risk of mental disorders. A low ability to cope with stress can also lead to mental health problems. People who have difficulty managing stress and regulating their emotions are more susceptible to mental disorders such as anxiety or depression.

SOCIAL FACTORS

Social factors play a significant role in mental health. A person's social environment, including family, friends, and community, can have a huge impact on their well-being. Positive social relationships and support can help reduce stress and promote emotional well-being. On the other hand, negative social relationships, such as conflict or social isolation, can increase the risk of mental disorders. Traumatic experiences such as abuse or neglect can also have long-term effects on mental health.

ENVIRONMENTAL FACTORS

Environmental factors can also affect mental health. An unfavorable environment, such as poverty, unemployment, or homelessness, can increase the risk of mental disorders. Stressful life events such as the loss of a loved one, a divorce, or financial problems can also lead to mental health problems. In addition, access to adequate health care and education, as well as the quality of the environment, can also play a role. A healthy environment, both physical and social, can promote well-being and reduce the risk of mental disorders.

LIFESTYLE FACTORS

Lifestyle factors also have an impact on mental health. A balanced diet, regular physical activity and sufficient sleep are important factors for well-being. An unhealthy diet, lack of exercise and lack of sleep can increase the risk of mental disorders. The use of alcohol, tobacco and drugs can also have negative effects on mental health. A healthy lifestyle that is aligned with the needs of the body and mind can help maintain and improve mental health.

CULTURAL FACTOR

Cultural factors play an important role in mental health. A person's cultural beliefs, values, and norms can influence their attitudes towards mental health and their willingness to seek help. Cultural differences can also affect the way mental disorders are perceived and treated. It is important to respect and consider cultural differences in order to ensure adequate support for people with mental health problems.

Overall, mental health is the result of a complex interaction between biological, psychological, social, environmental, and lifestyle factors. It's important to consider all of these factors and take a holistic approach to promoting mental health. By taking care of our physical and mental health, creating a supportive social environment, and maintaining a healthy lifestyle, we can strengthen our mental health and live fulfilling lives.

THE LINK BETWEEN PHYSICAL AND MENTAL HEALTH

The link between physical and mental health is an important aspect that is often overlooked. There is a close relationship between the state of our body and our mental well-being. In this section, we'll take a closer look at this relationship and explore the impact of physical health on mental health, as well as vice versa.

THE IMPACT OF PHYSICAL HEALTH ON MENTAL HEALTH

Our physical condition can have a significant impact on our mental health. When we feel physically healthy, we often have more energy, are more motivated, and feel better overall. Regular physical activity can help reduce stress, improve mood, and increase overall well-being.

Studies have shown that physical activity stimulates the production of endorphins, also known as "happiness hormones". These hormones can help reduce stress and promote positive emotions. In addition, regular exercise can improve the quality of sleep, which in turn can contribute to better mental health.

A healthy diet also plays an important role in our mental health. Eating balanced meals that are rich in nutrients can help reduce the risk of depression and anxiety. Certain nutrients such as omega-3 fatty acids, vitamin B12 and folic acid are particularly important for brain function and can have a positive effect on mood.

In addition, poor physical health can lead to increased stress, which in turn can lead to mental health problems. Chronic pain, illness, or injury can affect overall well-being and lead to anxiety, depression, or other mental disorders. It is therefore important to take care of our body and seek medical help if necessary.

THE IMPACT OF MENTAL HEALTH ON PHYSICAL HEALTH

In addition to physical health, mental health can also have a significant impact on our bodies. Stress, anxiety and depression can have a negative impact on the immune system and increase the risk of physical illness. Chronic stress, for example, can lead to increased blood pressure, heart problems, and a weakened immune system.

In addition, poor mental health can lead to unhealthy behaviors, which in turn can have a negative impact on the body. People who suffer from mental health problems often tend to consume unhealthy foods, abuse alcohol, or engage in less physical activity. These behaviors can lead to weight gain, cardiovascular disease, and other health problems.

It is important to note that the relationship between physical and mental health is an interaction. Good physical health can help improve mental health, and conversely, good mental health can help promote physical health. It is therefore important to consider both aspects and take a holistic approach to health.

By taking care of our bodies, exercising regularly, eating healthily, and seeking medical help when needed, we can improve our physical health while strengthening our mental health. Likewise, it is important to take care of our mental health, reduce stress, develop healthy coping mechanisms, and seek professional support when needed.

In the following chapters, we will take a closer look at different aspects of mental health and provide practical tips on how to promote holistic well-being. It is important to understand that mental health and physical health are closely related and that we should take care of both aspects equally in order to live a full and healthy life.

UNDERSTANDING MENTAL DISORDERS

THE DIFFERENT TYPES OF MENTAL DISORDERS

Mental disorders are prevalent and can affect people of all ages and social classes. They can affect a person's thinking, mood, and behavior, affecting their ability to perform everyday tasks. In this section, we will look at the different types of mental disorders to gain a better understanding of their diversity and impact.

ANXIETY

Anxiety disorders are one of the most common forms of mental disorders. They include various disorders such as generalized anxiety disorder, panic disorder, phobias, and social anxiety disorder. People with anxiety disorders experience excessive and uncontrollable fears or worries that can interfere with their daily lives. Symptoms may include physical discomfort such as palpitations, shortness of breath, sweating, and tremors.

MOOD DISORDERS

Mood disorders affect a person's emotional health and can lead to persistent changes in mood. The most common mood disorders include depression and bipolar disorder. People with depression often feel down, have low self-esteem, and lose interest in activities that used to bring them joy. In bipolar disorder, phases of depression alternate with phases of mania, in which the person is excessively energetic, euphoric and impulsive.

EATING DISORDERS

Eating disorders are mental disorders that affect a person's eating behavior and body image. The most common eating disorders include anorexia, bulimia, and binge eating disorder. People with anorexia have an excessive fear of gaining weight and keep their body weight low in unhealthy ways. In bulimia, sufferers suffer from repeated binge eating followed by weight control measures such as vomiting or excessive exercise. Binge eating disorder is the result of regular binge eating without any countermeasures being taken.

PERSONALITY DISORDERS

Personality disorders are long-term patterns of behaviors, thoughts, and emotions that deviate from the norm and can lead to problems in interpersonal relationships and daily life. There are several types of personality disorders, including borderline personality disorder, narcissistic personality disorder, and antisocial personality disorder. Each of these disorders has its own characteristics and effects on a person's behavior and interactions.

ADDICTIONS

Addictions are mental disorders characterized by the compulsive use of substances such as alcohol, drugs, or nicotine. People with addictions have difficulty controlling their use and experience withdrawal symptoms when they try to limit or stop use. Addictions can have a serious impact on a person's physical and mental health, affecting social life and job performance.

PSYCHOTIC DISORDERS

Psychotic disorders are serious mental illnesses that affect a person's thinking, perception, and behavior. Schizophrenia is one of the most common psychotic disorders. People with schizophrenia may experience hallucinations, delusions, disturbed thinking, and emotional flattening.

These disorders can significantly affect daily life and require intensive treatment.

This list of mental disorders is not exhaustive, as there are many more specific disorders that can affect a person's mental well-being. It is important to note that mental disorders are treatable and that there are various therapeutic approaches and support options available to help people with mental disorders live full and productive lives.

CAUSES OF MENTAL DISORDERS

Mental disorders can be caused by a variety of causes. It is important to understand that mental disorders do not arise from a single cause, but are often the result of a combination of factors. These factors can be biological, psychological, or social in nature. Here are some of the most common causes of mental disorders.

GENETIC FACTORS

Genetic predisposition plays a role in the development of mental disorders. Studies have shown that certain mental disorders, such as depression, anxiety disorders, and schizophrenia, have familial clusters. People whose family members suffer from a mental disorder are at increased risk of developing such a disorder themselves. This suggests that genetic factors may play a role in susceptibility to mental disorders.

NEUROCHEMICAL IMBALANCES

Mental disorders can also be caused by imbalances in the neurotransmitters in the brain. Neurotransmitters are chemical messengers that transmit information between nerve cells. An imbalance in these neurotransmitters, such as serotonin, dopamine or norepinephrine, can lead to disorders such as depression, anxiety disorders or bipolar disorder. Drugs that affect these neurotransmitters are often used to treat mental disorders.

EARLY LIFE EXPERIENCES

Early life experiences can have a significant impact on mental health. Traumatic events such as abuse, neglect, or the loss of a loved one can increase the risk of developing mental disorders. Children who grow up in an unstable or traumatic environment are at a higher risk of developing mental health problems in adulthood. Early life experiences can influence brain development and the regulation of stress responses.

PSYCHOSOCIAL FACTORS

Psychosocial factors such as stress, social isolation, financial problems, or stressful life events can increase the risk of mental disorders. Long-term stress can overload the nervous system and increase susceptibility to mental health problems. Social isolation and lack of social support can increase the risk of depression and anxiety disorders. Stressful life events such as the loss of a job, a separation, or the death of a loved one can also lead to mental disorders.

PERSONALITY TRAITS

Certain personality traits can increase the risk of mental disorders. People with low self-esteem, perfectionism, low frustration tolerance, or a high need for control may be more susceptible to mental health problems. These personality traits can lead to increased stress levels and make it difficult to cope with stressful situations.

SUBSTANCE ABUSE

Abuse of substances such as alcohol, drugs, or medication can lead to or worsen mental disorders. Long-term use of substances can affect the brain and neurotransmitters, leading to mood disorders, anxiety disorders or psychosis. People who already have a mental disorder are more susceptible to substance abuse than people without mental health problems.

It is important to note that these causes should not be considered in isolation. Often, they interact with each other and reinforce each other. A holistic view of the causes of mental disorders is crucial to develop appropriate treatment approaches and promote mental health.

SYMPTOMS AND DIAGNOSIS OF MENTAL DISORDERS

Mental disorders can manifest themselves in a variety of ways, causing a variety of symptoms. Symptoms can vary from person to person and depend on the type of disorder as well as individual factors. It is important to recognize the symptoms and make an accurate diagnosis to allow for appropriate treatment.

GENERAL SYMPTOMS OF MENTAL DISORDERS

Mental disorders can cause a variety of symptoms that can affect a person's thoughts, feelings, and behavior. Here are some common symptoms that can occur with various mental disorders:

Changes in thinking: A person with a mental disorder may have difficulty thinking clearly, concentrating, or making decisions. She may also have negative thoughts, worry constantly, or have unrealistic fears.

Changes in emotional state: Mental disorders can lead to severe mood swings. A person may feel sad, hopeless, anxious, irritable, or irritable. She may also experience the loss of interest in activities she once enjoyed.

Changes in behavior: Mental disorders can affect a person's behavior. She may withdraw, avoid social activities, or isolate herself. She may also exhibit unusual behaviors, such as aggression, self-harm, or substance abuse.

Physical symptoms: Some mental disorders can also cause physical symptoms, such as sleep disturbances, changes in appetite, fatigue, or physical discomfort without an identifiable medical cause.

DIAGNOSIS OF MENTAL DISORDERS

Diagnosing mental disorders requires a thorough evaluation of symptoms and a comprehensive medical history. As a rule, a specialist in psychiatry or a psychologist will make the diagnosis. Here are some steps that are commonly taken when diagnosing mental disorders:

Clinical evaluation: The doctor or psychologist will perform a detailed clinical evaluation to understand the symptoms and assess their impact on the person's daily life. This may include interviewing the person, their family, and possibly other loved ones.

Diagnostic criteria: The doctor or psychologist will compare the symptoms with the diagnostic criteria of the Diagnostic Manual of Mental Disorders (DSM-5). The DSM-5 is an internationally recognized classification system that facilitates the diagnosis of mental disorders.

Ruling out other causes: It is important to rule out other medical or psychological causes for the symptoms. This may include physical examinations, laboratory tests, or further psychological tests.

Differential diagnosis: In some cases, the symptoms of a mental disorder may be similar to those of other disorders. The doctor or psychologist will perform a differential diagnosis to rule out other possible causes and make the exact diagnosis.

Treatment plan: Once diagnosed, an individualized treatment plan is developed that is tailored to the specific needs of the person. This may include a combination of medication, psychotherapy, self-help strategies, and other supportive interventions.

Diagnosing mental disorders requires expertise and experience. It is important that the diagnosis is made by a qualified specialist or psychologist to ensure accurate and appropriate treatment.

THE IMPORTANCE OF EARLY DIAGNOSIS

Early diagnosis of mental disorders is crucial to initiate appropriate treatment and reduce the risk of complications. An untreated mental disorder can have a serious impact on a person's daily life and significantly affect their quality of life.

With early diagnosis, appropriate treatment measures can be taken to alleviate symptoms and improve mental health. This may include the use of medication, psychotherapy, self-help strategies, and other supportive measures.

In addition, early diagnosis can help the person be better informed and develop a better understanding of their symptoms and condition. This can help her deal with her mental disorder and develop coping strategies.

It is important to note that a diagnosis of mental disorders should not be stigmatized. Mental disorders are medical conditions that can be treated. Early diagnosis and appropriate treatment can help a person live a full and productive life.

In chapter Treatment Options for Mental Disorders, we will look at the different treatment options for mental disorders and how they can help improve mental health.

TREATMENT OPTIONS FOR MENTAL DISORDERS

Treating mental disorders is an important step on the path to mental health. There are different approaches and methods that can be used to help people with mental disorders. In this section, we will explore some of the most common treatment options for mental disorders.

PSYCHOTHERAPY

Psychotherapy is a widely used and effective method of treating mental disorders. It is based on conversations between the therapist and the patient and aims to identify and manage the underlying causes of the disorder. There are several types of psychotherapy, including cognitive behavioral therapy, psychodynamic therapy, and family therapy. Each of these forms of therapy has its own approaches and techniques, but the goal is always the same: to help the patient understand their thoughts, feelings, and behaviors and bring about positive change.

DRUG TREATMENT

In some cases, drug treatment may be needed to treat mental disorders. Psychotropic drugs are often used to treat depression, anxiety disorders, bipolar disorder, and other mental illnesses. These medications act on the brain and can help relieve symptoms and restore emotional balance. It is important to note that medication alone is usually not enough to treat mental disorders. They should always be used in combination with other forms of therapy such as psychotherapy.

SUPPORT GROUPS

Support groups are another way to treat mental disorders. In these groups, people who have had similar experiences meet to support each other and share experiences. Support groups provide a safe space for members to openly share their challenges and progress. By sharing stories and advice, members of the group can gain new perspectives and encourage each other. Support groups can be a valuable complement to other treatment methods and support the recovery process.

CLINICAL TREATMENT

In some cases, inpatient or outpatient clinical treatment may be required to treat mental disorders. This is especially the case if the symptoms are severe or endanger the patient's life. In a clinical setting, patients receive intensive care and support from a team of professionals, including doctors, therapists, and nursing staff. Clinical treatment can take various forms, such as inpatient admission to a psychiatric hospital or outpatient treatment in a day clinic. The goal of clinical treatment is to help patients manage their symptoms, regain their stability, and develop strategies for managing their condition.

ALTERNATIVE TREATMENT METHODS

In addition to traditional treatment methods, there are also alternative approaches to treating mental disorders. These include techniques such as acupuncture, yoga, meditation, and aromatherapy. Although there is limited scientific evidence on the effectiveness of these methods, some people report positive results. It is important to note that alternative treatments should not be seen as a substitute for conventional therapies, but rather as an adjunct to them. Before trying alternative treatments, one should consult with a professional and make sure they are safe and suitable.

Choosing the right method of treatment depends on the type and severity of the mental disorder. It is important for the patient to work with a professional to develop the best treatment strategy. A combination of psychotherapy, drug treatment, support groups, and clinical care can often be the most effective approach. Every person is unique, and therefore it may be necessary to try different approaches to find the best method of treatment. With the right support and treatment, people with mental disorders can live full and healthy lives.

STRESS MANAGEMENT AND EMOTIONAL WELL-BEING

WHAT IS STRESS AND HOW DOES IT AFFECT MENTAL HEALTH?

Stress is a natural reaction of the body to a challenge or strain. It is a normal reaction that helps us deal with difficult situations. However, stress can also have a negative impact on our mental health if it lasts for a long period of time or becomes too intense.

THE PHYSIOLOGICAL RESPONSE TO STRESS

When we are exposed to a stressful situation, the body releases stress hormones such as adrenaline and cortisol. These hormones prepare the body for a "fight or flight" response. This means that the body is put into a state of heightened alertness and activity to deal with the challenge.

The physiological response to stress includes increased heart rate, increased breathing, increased blood flow to the muscles, and increased concentration of blood sugar in the body. These reactions are designed to protect us in an acute stressful situation and increase our chances of survival.

ACUTE STRESS VS. CHRONIC STRESS

There are two types of stress: acute stress and chronic stress. Acute stress occurs when we are exposed to a short-term stress, such as an exam or an important project. Acute stress can motivate us and increase our performance.

Chronic stress, on the other hand, occurs when we are exposed to constant stress for a long period of time, such as professional pressures, financial problems or relationship problems. Chronic stress can lead to a variety of mental and physical health problems.

EFFECTS OF STRESS ON MENTAL HEALTH

Stress can affect mental health in a number of ways. Chronic stress can lead to anxiety, depression, sleep disorders, and increased susceptibility to mental disorders. Stress can also affect self-esteem and lead to a feeling of being overwhelmed and unable to cope with the demands of everyday life.

In addition, stress can also lead to a worsening of existing mental illnesses. People who already suffer from an anxiety disorder or depression are often more susceptible to the negative effects of stress.

COPING WITH STRESS FOR MENTAL HEALTH

It's important to manage stress effectively to maintain mental health. There are several stress management techniques that can help reduce stress levels and improve emotional well-being.

One way to manage stress is to develop healthy coping strategies such as regular physical activity, relaxation techniques such as meditation or yoga, getting enough sleep, and eating a balanced diet. These strategies can help lower stress levels and improve overall well-being.

It's also important to seek social support and talk to others about your feelings and stresses. Friends, family, or professional therapists can provide valuable support and help reduce stress.

THE LONG-TERM IMPACT OF STRESS ON MENTAL HEALTH

If stress persists for long periods of time and is not managed appropriately, it can lead to long-term mental health effects. Chronic stress can increase the risk of developing mental disorders such as anxiety disorders, depression, and burnout.

In addition, chronic stress can also lead to physical health problems such as cardiovascular disease, gastrointestinal problems, and a weakened immune system. It is therefore important to identify stress early and take appropriate measures to manage stress to avoid long-term effects on mental health.

Overall, stress is a natural part of life that can have both positive and negative effects. It's important to recognize stress, manage it appropriately, and develop healthy coping strategies to maintain mental health in the long term.

STRESS MANAGEMENT TECHNIQUES

Stress is a pervasive part of our modern lives. It can have various causes, such as job demands, financial burdens, interpersonal conflicts, or health problems. If stress is not managed adequately, it can lead to negative effects on our mental health. Fortunately, there are a variety of techniques that can help us manage stress effectively and improve our emotional well-being.

RELAXATION

A proven method of coping with stress is the use of relaxation techniques. These techniques help to calm the body and mind and achieve deep relaxation. Here are some popular relaxation techniques:

Progressive muscle relaxation

Progressive muscle relaxation is a technique in which different muscle groups are tensed one by one and then relaxed. Through this method, deep relaxation of the entire body is achieved. By focusing on the physical sensations, one can calm the mind and reduce stress.

Breathing

Breathing exercises are a simple and effective way to reduce stress. By breathing consciously, you can relax your body and calm your mind.

A popular breathing exercise is the so-called abdominal breathing, in which you breathe deeply into the abdomen and exhale slowly. This technique can help reduce stress and find inner peace.

Meditation

Meditation is a centuries-old practice that serves to calm the mind and achieve inner clarity. Through regular meditation, one can learn to rid the mind of disturbing thoughts and achieve deep relaxation. There are different types of meditation, such as mindfulness meditation, transcendental meditation, and guided meditation. Each of these techniques has its own benefits and can help reduce stress and improve emotional well-being.

EXERCISE AND PHYSICAL ACTIVITY

Exercise and physical activity are not only good for our bodies, but also for our mental health. Regular physical activity can help reduce stress and improve emotional well-being. Here are some ways exercise can help manage stress:

Endurance training

Endurance exercise, such as jogging, cycling, or swimming, can help reduce stress and improve emotional well-being. During exercise, endorphins are released, which act as natural stress reduction hormones. In addition, regular physical activity can help improve mood and boost self-esteem.

Yoga

Yoga is a holistic practice that connects body, mind and soul. By combining physical exercises, breathing techniques, and meditation, yoga can help reduce stress and improve emotional well-being. Yoga can also help improve the flexibility and strength of the body and correct posture.

Dance

Dancing is not only a fun activity, but also a great way to reduce stress and improve emotional well-being. Dancing releases endorphins, which provide a feeling of happiness and well-being. In addition, dancing can help boost self-confidence and improve body awareness.

COGNITIVE TECHNIQUES

Cognitive techniques are strategies that aim to identify and change negative thought patterns. By replacing negative thoughts with positive and realistic thoughts, one can reduce stress and improve emotional well-being. Here are some cognitive techniques for managing stress:

Restructuring of Thoughts

Mind restructuring is about recognizing negative thought patterns and replacing them with positive and realistic thoughts. By questioning negative thoughts and taking alternative perspectives, one can reduce stress and improve emotional well-being. For example, you can replace negative self-talk like "I can't do this" with positive self-talk like "I can do my best."

Mindfulness

Mindfulness is a technique that involves focusing on the present moment and consciously perceiving without judgment. Through regular mindfulness exercises, one can learn to calm the mind and reduce stress. Mindfulness can also help identify and change negative thought patterns.

Relaxation techniques for the mind

Relaxation techniques for the mind, such as visualization or autogenic training, can help reduce stress and improve emotional well-being. By imagining pleasant images or repeating soothing words, one can calm the mind and achieve deep relaxation.

The stress management techniques mentioned above are just a few examples. Every person is unique and it can be helpful to try different techniques to see which one suits you best. By regularly using stress management techniques, one can strengthen one's mental health and achieve better emotional well-being.

EMOTIONAL WELL-BEING AND ITS IMPORTANCE

Emotional well-being plays a crucial role in our mental health. It refers to our emotional state, mood, and overall sense of well-being. When we feel good emotionally, we are able to better cope with life's challenges and live a full and happy life.

THE IMPORTANCE OF EMOTIONAL WELL-BEING

Emotional well-being is closely linked to our mental health. It affects our way of thinking, our relationships, our performance, and our overall quality of life. When we feel good emotionally, we are able to better manage stress, build positive relationships, and achieve our goals.

Good emotional well-being also allows us to deal with and regulate negative emotions. It helps us to understand ourselves and recognize our own needs and limitations. When we feel emotionally comfortable, we are able to accept ourselves and love ourselves, which in turn leads to positive self-esteem.

EMOTIONAL INTELLIGENCE

An important aspect of emotional well-being is emotional intelligence. Emotional intelligence refers to our ability to recognize, understand, and regulate our own emotions, as well as recognize other people's emotions and respond to them empathetically.

People with high emotional intelligence are able to effectively regulate and manage their emotions. They can also recognize other people's emotions and respond appropriately to them. This allows them to build healthy relationships and resolve conflicts constructively.

WAYS TO PROMOTE EMOTIONAL WELL-BEING

There are several ways to promote and improve emotional well-being. Here are some practical tips:

1. Self-reflection: Take regular time to reflect on and understand your own emotions. Ask yourself what makes you happy, what makes you sad, and what makes you anxious. This will help you get to know yourself better and identify your own needs.
2. Find ways to express yourself: Find healthy ways to express your emotions. This can be done by writing in a journal, painting, listening to music, or talking to familiar people. Expressing emotions can help you process them and feel better.
3. Self-care: Take time for yourself and do things that bring you joy. This can be reading a book, meeting friends, pursuing a hobby, or relaxing in nature. Self-care is important to recharge your emotional batteries and take care of your well-being.
4. Seek social support: Seek support from trusted people such as friends, family, or a therapist. Sharing your emotions and challenges with others can help you feel understood and supported.
5. Practice mindfulness: Mindfulness is a technique in which you focus on the present moment and observe your emotions and thoughts without judgment. Through regular mindfulness exercises, you can learn to better regulate your emotions and deal with stress.
6. Cultivate positive relationships: Invest time and energy in healthy relationships. Surround yourself with people who support you, respect you, and give you positive energy. Healthy relationships can boost your emotional well-being and help you feel happier and more fulfilled.

The impact of stress on emotional well-being

Stress can have a significant impact on our emotional well-being. Chronic stress can lead to anxiety, depression, and other mental disorders. It's important to recognize stress and develop effective coping strategies to protect emotional well-being.

Stress reduction techniques such as relaxation exercises, physical activity, and learning stress management techniques can help improve emotional well-being and reduce stress. It's also important to develop healthy coping mechanisms, such as achieving a good work-life balance, setting realistic goals, and prioritizing self-care.

THE ROLE OF MINDFULNESS IN STRESS MANAGEMENT

Mindfulness is an effective way to manage stress and promote emotional well-being. By practicing mindfulness, we learn to be aware of the present moment consciously, without judgment and with acceptance.

Mindfulness can help us detach ourselves from burdensome thoughts and worries and focus on the here and now. By being mindful, we can better regulate our emotions and deal with stress. Mindfulness can also help improve our relationships by being present and attentive.

There are several mindfulness exercises that you can incorporate into your daily routine, such as breathing exercises, body scanning, meditation, and mindful eating. Through regular practice, you can strengthen your mindfulness skills and improve your emotional well-being.

Overall, emotional well-being is of great importance to our mental health. By taking care of our emotional well-being and developing effective coping strategies, we can live a full and happy life. It's important to understand yourself, take care of yourself, and seek support when needed.

WAYS TO PROMOTE EMOTIONAL WELL-BEING

Emotional well-being plays a crucial role in our mental health. It refers to our state of happiness, contentment, and inner balance. Strong emotional well-being can help us cope with stress, build positive relationships, and improve our quality of life. In this section, we will explore different ways to promote emotional well-being.

SELF-REFLECTION AND MINDFULNESS

An important way to promote emotional well-being is through self-reflection. By being aware of our thoughts, feelings, and needs, we can develop a deeper understanding of ourselves. This allows us to recognize our strengths and weaknesses and to be more aware of our actions and decisions.

The practice of mindfulness is closely related to self-reflection. It involves consciously observing and accepting the present moment without judging or judging it. Through regular mindfulness exercises such as meditation or breathing techniques, we can learn to be present in the here and now and better regulate our emotions.

POSITIVE SELF-TALK AND AFFIRMATIONS

Our thoughts have a huge impact on our emotional well-being. Negative self-talk and self-critical thoughts can weigh us down and affect our self-esteem. One way to counteract this is through the practice of positive self-talk and affirmations.

Positive self-talk involves consciously replacing negative thoughts with positive and supportive statements. By encouraging ourselves and acknowledging positive qualities, we boost our self-confidence and promote a positive self-image.

Affirmations are short, positive phrases that we repeat regularly to influence our subconscious. By giving ourselves positive messages, we can break negative thought patterns and improve our emotional well-being.

SOCIAL SUPPORT AND INTERPERSONAL RELATIONSHIPS

The quality of our interpersonal relationships has a huge impact on our emotional well-being. Sharing positive emotions, support, and understanding with other people can help us reduce stress and feel better.

It's important to seek social support and build healthy relationships. This can be achieved by building friendships, sharing feelings and needs with trusted people, and participating in social activities. By connecting with others and supporting each other, we can strengthen our emotional well-being.

PHYSICAL ACTIVITY AND HEALTHY EATING

The effects of physical activity and healthy eating on our emotional well-being are well documented. Regular physical activity can promote the release of endorphins, also known as "happiness hormones," and reduce stress. It can also help improve our mood and boost self-esteem.

A balanced diet rich in nutrients can also have a positive impact on our emotional well-being. Eating fresh fruits and vegetables, whole grains, healthy fats, and enough water can help boost our energy and stabilize our mood.

HOBBIES AND CREATIVE EXPRESSIONS

Engaging in hobbies and creative activities can be a valuable way to boost our emotional well-being. By engaging in activities that bring us joy and fulfillment, we can reduce stress and experience positive emotions.

Whether it's painting, writing, making music, or gardening, immersing ourselves in creative processes can help us express our feelings and connect with our inner selves. It also allows us to leave everyday life behind and focus on positive experiences.

RELAXATION TECHNIQUES AND STRESS RELIEF

Relaxation techniques are an important part of promoting emotional well-being. They help us reduce stress, calm our minds, and relax our bodies. Effective relaxation techniques include breathing exercises, progressive muscle relaxation, yoga, and meditation.

By regularly incorporating relaxation techniques into our daily lives, we can reduce our stress responses and improve our ability to manage stress. This allows us to recover better and promote our emotional well-being.

Promoting emotional well-being requires a conscious effort and regular practice. By focusing on these pathways and incorporating them into our daily lives, we can strengthen our emotional well-being and achieve better mental health.

THE IMPACT OF STRESS ON EMOTIONAL WELL-BEING

Stress is a pervasive part of our modern lives. All of us struggle with stress in some form, whether it's due to work, relationships, financial problems, or other challenges. However, stress can not only affect our bodies, but also our emotional well-being.

THE EFFECTS OF STRESS ON EMOTIONAL WELL-BEING

Stress can have a variety of negative effects on our emotional well-being. When we are stressed, we often feel overwhelmed, anxious, and irritable. Our thoughts can constantly revolve around the stress-inducing situations, which leads to increased tension and restlessness. This can lead to an impairment of our mood and our ability to feel joy and contentment.

In addition, chronic stress can lead to a variety of mental disorders, such as anxiety disorders, depression, and burnout. When we are exposed to high levels of stress for long periods of time, it can lead to the depletion of our psychological resources and affect our ability to cope with the demands of everyday life.

STRESS MANAGEMENT AND EMOTIONAL WELL-BEING

Managing stress is crucial to our emotional well-being. By learning to manage stress and develop effective stress management strategies, we can strengthen our mental health and improve our emotional well-being.

An important stress management strategy is to identify and change stress-inducing thoughts and beliefs. Often, it is negative thought patterns and unrealistic expectations that lead to increased stress levels. By recognizing these thought patterns and replacing negative thoughts with positive and realistic beliefs, we can reduce our stress and increase our emotional well-being.

In addition, it is important to integrate effective stress management techniques into our daily lives. These include, for example, relaxation exercises such as meditation, breathing techniques and progressive muscle relaxation. These techniques can help us reduce stress, calm our minds, and regulate our emotions.

THE IMPACT OF MINDFULNESS ON EMOTIONAL WELL-BEING

Another important method for managing stress and promoting emotional well-being is the practice of mindfulness. Mindfulness means being consciously in the present moment and noticing our thoughts, feelings, and bodily sensations without judgment.

By being mindful, we can detach ourselves from stressful thoughts and worries and focus on the here and now. This can help us reduce our stress levels and improve our emotional well-being. Studies have shown that regular mindfulness practice can lead to a reduction in stress, anxiety, and depression.

There are several ways to integrate mindfulness into our everyday lives. These include, for example, regular meditation, conscious eating, mindful breathing and the conscious experience of activities such as walking or yoga. By practicing these practices regularly, we can strengthen our ability to manage stress and promote our emotional well-being.

THE IMPORTANCE OF SELF-CARE IN STRESS MANAGEMENT

In addition to mindfulness practice, self-care is also an important aspect of managing stress and promoting emotional well-being. Self-care means taking good care of yourself and consciously taking time out to relax and recharge.

By lovingly caring for ourselves, we can reduce our stress levels and improve our emotional well-being. This can include regularly scheduling time for ourselves, setting healthy boundaries, recognizing and meeting our needs, and indulging in positive activities.

It is important to realize that self-care is not a selfish act, but a necessary measure to maintain our mental health. By taking good care of ourselves, we can better manage stress, strengthen our resilience and promote our emotional well-being in the long term.

Overall, stress has a significant impact on our emotional well-being. By incorporating effective stress management strategies such as mindfulness and self-care into our daily lives, we can reduce our stress and improve our emotional well-being. It's important to consciously take time for yourself and pay attention to the needs of our minds and bodies to promote long-term mental health.

THE ROLE OF MINDFULNESS IN STRESS MANAGEMENT

Mindfulness is a practice that has become increasingly important in recent years when it comes to managing stress and promoting mental health. It is based on the idea that we consciously focus on the present moment and observe our thoughts, feelings, and physical sensations without judgment.

WHAT IS MINDFULNESS?

Mindfulness is a form of meditation that has its origins in the Buddhist tradition. However, it has been adopted by many psychological approaches and has been widely used in Western cultures. Mindfulness practice is about calming the mind and focusing on the present moment without being distracted by thoughts or emotions.

HOW DOES MINDFULNESS AFFECT STRESS MANAGEMENT?

Mindfulness can be an effective way to reduce stress and improve mental health. By focusing on the present moment and observing our thoughts and emotions, we can learn to deal with stressors in a healthy and constructive way. Through the practice of mindfulness, we can slow down our reactions to stressors and act more consciously.

MINDFULNESS EXERCISES FOR STRESS MANAGEMENT

There are several mindfulness exercises that can help with stress management. One of the most well-known exercises is breathing meditation. We focus on our breath and observe it without controlling it. This exercise helps us calm the mind and focus on the present moment.

Another exercise is body awareness. In doing so, we consciously perceive our physical sensations without judging or changing them. This exercise helps us connect with our body and become aware of how we feel.

Another mindfulness exercise is conscious eating. We take time to consciously enjoy our meals and fully perceive each bite. This exercise helps us focus on the moment and sharpen our senses.

INTEGRATING MINDFULNESS INTO EVERYDAY LIFE

Mindfulness can not only be practiced through formal exercises, but can also be integrated into everyday life. By consciously focusing on our actions and thoughts, we can live more mindfully. For example, we can consciously do our daily tasks, such as brushing our teeth or washing dishes. By focusing on these activities and not letting our mind wander, we can fully experience the moment and reduce stress.

THE BENEFITS OF MINDFULNESS IN MANAGING STRESS

The practice of mindfulness can have many benefits for stress management and mental health. By becoming more mindful, we can better control our responses to stressors and become more aware of our needs and limitations. Mindfulness can also help identify and change negative thought patterns, which can lead to a more positive attitude and better emotional well-being.

In addition, mindfulness can also improve concentration and memory, strengthen relationships, and increase overall life satisfaction. By consciously focusing on the present moment, we can experience life more intensely and connect with ourselves and our surroundings.

RESULT

Mindfulness plays an important role in managing stress and promoting mental health. Through the practice of mindfulness, we can learn to consciously experience the present moment and deal with stressors in a healthy and constructive way. By becoming more mindful, we can better control our responses to stressors and improve our emotional well-being. Incorporating mindfulness into everyday life can have many positive effects on our mental health and help us live a full and stress-free life.

SELF-CARE AND SELF-ESTEEM

THE IMPORTANCE OF SELF-CARE FOR MENTAL HEALTH

Mental health is a precious commodity that we should all protect and nurture. An important component of maintaining mental health is self-care. Self-care refers to consciously and actively caring for one's well-being on a physical, emotional, and mental level. It's about giving yourself time, attention, and love to promote your health and happiness.

THE IMPORTANCE OF SELF-CARE

Self-care is crucial for mental health because it helps us take care of our own needs and respect ourselves. By taking care of ourselves, we can recharge our energy and resources, reduce stress, and create balance in our lives. Self-care also allows us to recognize and respect our own boundaries, which can protect us from overwork and burnout.

When we neglect ourselves and ignore our own needs, we can feel exhausted, stressed, and unhappy. This can lead to various mental health problems such as anxiety, depression, and sleep disorders. However, by taking care of ourselves on a regular basis, we can strengthen our mental health and live a full and happy life.

PRACTICAL TIPS FOR SELF-CARE

There are many different ways we can incorporate self-care into our daily lives. Here are some practical tips that can help you boost your mental health:

Prioritize your needs: Take the time to figure out what's good for you and what you need to feel comfortable. Set clear boundaries and say "no" when you're overworked.

Take care of your physical health: Get enough sleep, eat a healthy diet, and get regular physical activity. Also pay attention to your hygiene and treat yourself to regular relaxation periods.

Find time to relax: discover activities that bring you joy and help you reduce stress. This can be, for example, reading a book, listening to music, painting, or practicing yoga.

Maintain social relationships: Spend time with your loved ones and nurture your relationships. Share your feelings and worries with others and seek support when you need it.

Practice mindfulness: Be present in the present moment and pay attention to your thoughts, feelings, and body sensations. Make time for meditation or other mindfulness exercises on a regular basis.

Do things that bring you joy: Make time for hobbies and activities that you enjoy and fulfill. This can be reading, cooking, dancing, or gardening.

Seek professional support: If you feel that your mental health is compromised, do not hesitate to seek professional help. A therapist or psychiatrist can help you overcome your challenges and improve your mental health.

BOOST SELF-ESTEEM

An important aspect of self-care is strengthening self-esteem. Self-esteem refers to the appreciation and respect we feel for ourselves. Healthy self-esteem is crucial for our mental health, as it helps us accept ourselves, love ourselves, and trust ourselves.

To boost self-esteem, it's important to have positive self-talk and focus on our strengths and successes. It can also be helpful to identify negative self-images and self-doubt and work to overcome them. Cultivating self-care and acknowledging our own needs also help boost our self-esteem.

SELF-ACCEPTANCE AND SELF-LOVE

Another important aspect of self-care is self-acceptance and self-love. Self-acceptance means accepting yourself as you are, with all your strengths and weaknesses. It's about allowing yourself to be human and making mistakes without judging yourself.

Self-love refers to the ability to love oneself unconditionally and treat oneself with kindness and compassion. It's about respecting yourself, forgiving yourself, and supporting yourself, regardless of external circumstances or opinions of others.

Developing self-acceptance and self-love takes time and practice. It can be helpful to repeat positive affirmations, practice self-care rituals, and consciously remind ourselves that we deserve to be loved and appreciated—both by others and by ourselves.

Overall, self-care is an essential part of mental health. By taking care of ourselves, we can strengthen our mental health, reduce stress, and live a full and happy life. Take time for yourself, listen to your needs, and treat yourself with love and respect. You deserve to take good care of yourself.

PRACTICAL TIPS FOR SELF-CARE

Self-care is an important aspect of mental health. It's about respecting yourself, taking care of yourself, and taking care of your well-being. Often we neglect ourselves and focus too much on the needs of others. But in order to stay mentally healthy in the long term, it is essential to regularly take time for yourself and take care of your own needs. In this section, we'll share practical self-care tips that can help you boost your mental health.

TAKE TIME FOR YOURSELF

One of the most important ways to take care of yourself is to take time for yourself on a regular basis. In our hectic everyday lives, we often forget to take a break and relax. Consciously take time for yourself to recharge your batteries. This may mean making time for hobbies, reading a book, going for a walk, or just relaxing. By taking time for yourself on a regular basis, you can reduce stress and increase your well-being.

SETTING HEALTHY BOUNDARIES

It's important to set healthy boundaries and know when to say "no." Often, we feel obligated to live up to the expectations of others and to burden ourselves excessively. But this can lead to overload and stress. Learn to recognize and respect your own needs. Set clear boundaries and communicate them openly and honestly. By respecting your own boundaries, you can protect your mental health and create balance in your life.

DEVELOP A SELF-CARE ROUTINE

A regular self-care routine can help you take care of yourself and promote your well-being. Make time for activities that bring you joy and give you energy. This can be, for example, a relaxing bath, a massage, listening to your favorite music or engaging in a creative activity. Find out what is good for you and integrate these activities into your everyday life. By scheduling time for self-care on a regular basis, you can boost your mental health and take better care of yourself.

SEEK SUPPORT

It's important to realize that it's okay to ask for support and accept help. Often we try to do everything on our own and carry a heavy burden on our shoulders. But it is important to know that there are people who want to support us. Find trusted friends, family members, or professional help if you need support. By getting support, you can boost your mental health and take better care of yourself.

PRACTICING MINDFULNESS

Mindfulness is a technique that can help you be present in the present moment and be aware of your thoughts and feelings without judging or judging them. By incorporating mindfulness into your daily routine, you can reduce stress and increase your well-being. Make time for mindfulness exercises such as meditation, breathing exercises or yoga on a regular basis. By being mindful, you can strengthen your mental health and take better care of yourself.

GET ENOUGH SLEEP

Sleep is an important factor in mental health. It's important to get enough sleep to recover and recharge your batteries. Be sure to develop regular sleep habits and create a relaxing sleep environment. Avoid caffeine and electronic devices before bed so as not to disturb your sleep. By getting enough sleep, you can boost your mental health and take better care of yourself.

ENGAGE IN POSITIVE SELF-TALK

The way we talk to ourselves can have a huge impact on our mental health. Often, we tend to be critical of ourselves and engage in negative self-talk. But it's important to have positive self-talk and treat yourself with kindness and compassion. Pay attention to your inner dialogues and try to replace negative thoughts with positive and supportive thoughts. By engaging in positive self-talk, you can boost your self-esteem and take better care of yourself.

STRESS REDUCTION THROUGH PHYSICAL ACTIVITY

Physical activity is not only good for the body, but also for mental health. Exercise releases endorphins, which provide a feeling of well-being and happiness. Find a form of physical activity that you enjoy and that you can do regularly. This can be, for example, jogging, dancing, swimming or yoga. By being physically active on a regular basis, you can reduce stress and boost your mental health.

SPENDING TIME IN NATURE

Nature has a calming effect on the psyche. Take time to be in nature and enjoy the beauty of the surroundings. Go for a walk, have picnics in the park or spend time in the garden. By spending time in nature, you can reduce stress and increase your well-being.

EAT HEALTHY

A balanced diet can have a huge impact on mental health. Make sure to eat a healthy diet and eat enough fruits, vegetables, whole grains, and healthy fats. Avoid excessive consumption of sugary foods and processed foods. By eating healthily, you can boost your mental health and take better care of yourself.

These practical self-care tips can help you boost your mental health and take better care of yourself. Take time for yourself, set healthy boundaries, seek support, practice mindfulness, get enough sleep, engage in positive self-talk, engage in physical activity, spend time in nature, and eat healthily. By incorporating these tips into your daily routine, you can boost your mental health in the long term.

BOOST SELF-ESTEEM

Self-esteem plays a crucial role in our mental health. It affects how we perceive ourselves, how we deal with challenges, and how we behave in relationships with other people. Healthy self-esteem is therefore of great importance in order to live a full and happy life.

THE IMPORTANCE OF SELF-ESTEEM

Self-esteem refers to the evaluation and appreciation of our own person. It is the feeling that we love, accept, and value ourselves, regardless of our flaws, weaknesses, or successes. Strong self-esteem allows us to trust ourselves, make decisions, and pursue our goals.

Healthy self-esteem has many positive effects on our lives. It helps us to respect ourselves and value ourselves. It allows us to distance ourselves from other people's negative influences and not be influenced by their opinion of us. Strong self-esteem also promotes our psychological resilience and helps us cope better with stress and challenges.

WAYS TO BOOST SELF-ESTEEM

There are several ways to boost self-esteem and build a healthy self-image. Here are some practical tips that can help you:

Positive self-talk

One way to boost self-esteem is to engage in positive self-talk. Encourage yourself, remind yourself of your strengths and successes, and allow yourself to make mistakes and learn from them. Avoid negative self-talk and remember that no one is perfect.

Self-care

Self-care plays an important role in boosting self-esteem. Take time for yourself and do things that bring you joy. Take care of your physical health by getting enough sleep, eating a healthy diet, and exercising regularly. By treating yourself well, you show yourself that you are worthy of being treated well.

Celebrating success

Celebrate your successes, no matter how small they may be. Take time to acknowledge your progress and be proud of yourself. Not only does this boost your self-esteem, but it also motivates you to keep striving for your goals.

Accepting Yourself

Accept yourself as you are, with all your strengths and weaknesses. No one is perfect, and that's okay. Allow yourself to be human and make mistakes. Accepting oneself means loving and accepting oneself unconditionally.

Surrounding yourself with positive people

Surround yourself with people who support you and are good for you. Avoid people who bring you down or make you feel inferior. Surround yourself with positive influences that boost your self-esteem and encourage you to reach your full potential.

THE EFFECTS OF HEALTHY SELF-ESTEEM

Healthy self-esteem has many positive effects on our lives. It allows us to appear confident and self-assured, pursue our goals, and achieve our dreams. People with strong self-esteem often have better relationships with other people because they can love and accept themselves.

Healthy self-esteem also helps us cope better with stress and challenges. It strengthens our psychological resilience and allows us to accept setbacks as part of life and learn from them. People with strong self-esteem are often more optimistic and have a more positive outlook on life.

SELF-ESTEEM AND MENTAL HEALTH

Self-esteem plays a crucial role in our mental health. People with low self-esteem are more susceptible to mental disorders such as depression, anxiety disorders, and eating disorders. Healthy self-esteem can help reduce these risks and maintain good mental health.

It is important to note that boosting self-esteem is an ongoing process. It takes time, patience and self-reflection. Be patient with yourself and give yourself permission to evolve and grow. By boosting your self-esteem, you are investing in your mental health and well-being.

SELF-ACCEPTANCE AND SELF-LOVE

Self-acceptance and self-love play a crucial role in our mental health. It's about accepting ourselves, with all our strengths and weaknesses, and loving yourself unconditionally. Self-acceptance means accepting yourself as you are without constantly comparing yourself to others or criticizing yourself. Self-love means respecting yourself, taking care of yourself, and valuing yourself.

WHY IS SELF-ACCEPTANCE IMPORTANT?

Self-acceptance is important because it helps us develop healthy self-esteem. When we accept ourselves, we feel valuable and lovable, regardless of our flaws or imperfections. This positive self-image boosts our confidence and resilience, which makes us better empowered to deal with life's challenges.

In addition, self-acceptance allows us to be authentic and stay true to ourselves. When we accept ourselves, we don't have to constantly pretend or try to live up to the expectations of others. We can recognize our own needs and desires and follow them without feeling guilty or insecure.

HOW TO DEVELOP SELF-ACCEPTANCE?

Developing self-acceptance takes time and practice. Here are some steps that can help you develop self-acceptance:

Self-reflection: Take time to reflect on yourself and identify your strengths and weaknesses. Accept that no one is perfect and that flaws and weaknesses are part of being human.

Positive self-talk: Replace negative self-talk with positive and supportive thoughts. Encourage yourself and remind yourself that you are valuable and lovable.

Self-care: Take care of yourself and make time for activities that bring you joy. Pay attention to your needs and set clear boundaries to protect yourself.

Forgiveness: Forgive yourself for past mistakes and let go of negative feelings. No one is flawless, and it's important to forgive yourself in order to move forward.

Acceptance of change: Accept that change is a natural part of life and that you will evolve and grow over time. Be patient with yourself and give yourself space for personal growth.

WHAT IS SELF-LOVE?

Self-love is the ability to love oneself unconditionally and treat oneself with kindness and compassion. It's about respecting yourself and valuing yourself, regardless of external circumstances or opinions of others.

WHY IS SELF-LOVE IMPORTANT?

Self-love is important because it helps us develop healthy self-esteem and prioritize ourselves. When we love ourselves, we acknowledge our own worth and set clear boundaries to protect ourselves from negative influences. This boosts our confidence and ability to build healthy relationships.

In addition, self-love allows us to take care of ourselves and take care of our own well-being. We take time for self-care and pay attention to our physical, emotional, and spiritual needs. This helps us to live a balanced and fulfilling life.

HOW TO DEVELOP SELF-LOVE?

Developing self-love requires self-reflection and conscious choices. Here are some steps that can help you develop self-love:

Self-acceptance: Accept yourself with all your strengths and weaknesses. Allow yourself to be human and make mistakes without judging yourself.

Self-care: Make time for self-care and do things that bring you joy. Pay attention to your needs and set clear boundaries to protect yourself.

Positive self-talk: Speak to yourself with kindness and compassion. Remind yourself that you are valuable and lovable, regardless of external circumstances or opinions of others.

Forgiveness: Forgive yourself for past mistakes and let go of negative feelings. Allow yourself to move forward and evolve.

Self-acceptance in relationships: Choose relationships that support your self-love and encourage you to be your best self. Avoid relationships that drag you down or interfere with your self-love.

Developing self-acceptance and self-love is a lifelong process. It requires patience, self-reflection, and a willingness to change yourself. But it's worth it, because self-acceptance and self-love are key to strong mental health and a fulfilling life.

RELATIONSHIPS AND SOCIAL SUPPORT

THE IMPORTANCE OF RELATIONSHIPS FOR MENTAL HEALTH

Relationships play a crucial role in our mental health. They affect our well-being, our mood and our quality of life. Humans are social creatures by nature and contact with other people is of great importance to us. Good relationships can support us, empower us, and make us feel like we're not alone.

THE IMPORTANCE OF SOCIAL TIES

Social bonds are fundamental to our mental health. They give us a sense of belonging and cohesion. When we have close relationships with other people, we feel supported and loved. These relationships can help us navigate difficult times and give us a sense of security.

Studies have shown that people with strong social ties have better mental health. They are less susceptible to mental disorders such as depression and anxiety. Social support can also help reduce stress and improve overall well-being.

BUILDING AND MAINTAINING HEALTHY RELATIONSHIPS

Building and maintaining healthy relationships takes time, effort, and communication. It is important to actively work to develop and maintain good relationships. Here are some tips on how to build and maintain healthy relationships:

Communication: Open and honest communication is key to a healthy relationship. Take time to listen and express your thoughts and feelings. Avoid piling things up or assuming that the other person knows your needs.

Trust: Trust is an important part of any relationship. Make an effort to build trust by keeping your promises and being honest and reliable. Trust is a process that takes time to grow.

Support: Show interest and support for each other's needs and goals. Be there to help and encourage when your partner or friends need support. A supportive relationship can help reduce stress and increase well-being.

Conflict resolution: Conflict is inevitable in any relationship. It is important to approach conflicts constructively and to look for solutions that are acceptable to both sides. Respect each other's opinions and feelings and seek compromises.

Spend time together: Take time to do activities together and create memories. Shared experiences can strengthen the bond and deepen the feeling of connection.

THE IMPACT OF SOCIAL SUPPORT ON MENTAL HEALTH

Social support plays an important role in our mental health. When we feel supported by other people, we are better able to cope with stress and are less prone to mental disorders. Social support can come in a variety of forms, such as:

Emotional support: Feeling that someone is there for us and listening to us can help us deal with emotional challenges. It can make us feel like we're not alone and that we have support when we need it.

Instrumental support: Practical help from other people can help us deal with the demands of everyday life. For example, friends or family members can help us cope with tasks or problems.

Information support: Information and advice from other people can help us make better decisions and orient ourselves in difficult situations. Sharing information can also help us gain new perspectives and better understand our problems.

Social support can come from a variety of sources, such as family, friends, colleagues, or support groups. It's important to build and maintain a network of supportive relationships to boost our mental health.

DEALING WITH CONFLICTS IN RELATIONSHIPS

Conflict is a natural part of relationships. It is important to learn how to approach and resolve conflicts constructively in order to maintain and strengthen the relationship. Here are some tips on how to deal with conflict in relationships:

Communication: Talk openly and honestly about your feelings and needs. Listen actively and try to understand each other's perspective. Avoid blaming or blaming the other.

Willingness to compromise: Be willing to compromise and look for solutions that are acceptable to both sides. Focus on common goals and interests instead of insisting on your own points of view.

Respect: Respect each other's opinions and feelings, even if you disagree. Avoid making derogatory or hurtful comments. Conflicts should be resolved in a respectful and constructive manner.

Take time: Take time to cool down and think before reacting to a conflict. Sometimes it's helpful to take a break and come back to the topic later when the emotions have subsided.

Seek professional help: If conflicts in relationships seem chronic or insurmountable, it may be helpful to seek professional help. A therapist or counselor can help you identify the underlying issues and find solutions.

Conflict is normal and can even help strengthen relationships if approached constructively. It is important to look at conflict as a way to grow and improve the relationship.

BUILDING AND MAINTAINING HEALTHY RELATIONSHIPS

Healthy relationships play a crucial role in our mental health. They offer us support, understanding, love and security. In this section, we'll look at how to build and maintain healthy relationships to promote well-being.

THE IMPORTANCE OF COMMUNICATION IN RELATIONSHIPS

Good communication is the foundation of any healthy relationship. It allows us to express our thoughts, feelings, and needs while understanding each other's. Through open and honest communication, misunderstandings can be avoided and conflicts resolved. It is important to listen actively and treat the other person with respect. Through clear and respectful communication, we can build trust in a relationship and build a deeper connection.

COMMON INTERESTS AND ACTIVITIES

Shared interests and activities are another important aspect of healthy relationships. By sharing common hobbies, interests, or activities, we can share positive experiences with each other and strengthen our bond. It's important to spend time together and create shared experiences. This may mean setting aside time for each other on a regular basis or planning activities together. By sharing positive experiences, we can deepen our relationship and strengthen the feeling of connection.

TRUST AND RELIABILITY

Trust and reliability are fundamental elements of healthy relationships. Trust means that we can rely on the other person and feel safe that he or she respects our needs and boundaries. Reliability means that we keep our promises and are there for others when they need us. By building trust and reliability in a relationship, we create a secure and stable foundation on which we can support each other.

CONFLICTING CONSTRUCTIVE PASSWORD

Conflict is inevitable in any relationship. However, it is important to resolve conflicts constructively so as not to put a strain on the relationship. This means that we communicate openly and respectfully with each other and try to find a solution that is acceptable to both sides. It is important to respond to the other person and understand their perspective. By dealing constructively with conflicts, we can strengthen our relationship and deepen our trust in each other.

SETTING AND RESPECTING BOUNDARIES

Setting boundaries is an important part of healthy relationships. It is important to know our own needs and boundaries and to communicate them clearly and respectfully. At the same time, it is important to respect each other's boundaries and acknowledge their needs. By setting and respecting boundaries, we create a healthy dynamic in the relationship and protect ourselves from being overwhelmed or exploited.

SUPPORT AND EMPATHY

Support and empathy are crucial for healthy relationships. By supporting each other and being empathetic to each other's needs, we can build a deep connection. It is important to listen to the other person, encourage them and offer them help when needed. Through support and empathy, we can strengthen trust and connection in a relationship.

TIME FOR YOURSELF AND INDIVIDUAL FREEDOM

Although healthy relationships are important, it's also important to have time for yourself and enjoy individual freedom. Every person needs time and space to pursue their own interests and develop themselves. By making time for self-care and personal growth, we can enrich our relationships while promoting our own mental health.

SEEK PROFESSIONAL HELP

Sometimes relationships can be difficult and it can be helpful to seek professional help. A therapist or counsellor can support us in reflecting on our relationship, resolving conflicts and finding new ways of being together. It's important to realize that there's no shame in seeking professional help, and that it can be a sign of strength and commitment to the relationship.

Healthy relationships are an important part of our mental health. By maintaining good communication, sharing common interests, building trust, resolving conflicts constructively, setting and respecting boundaries, showing support and empathy, having time for ourselves, and seeking professional help when needed, we can build and maintain healthy and fulfilling relationships. These relationships help strengthen our emotional well-being and provide us with support during difficult times.

THE IMPACT OF SOCIAL SUPPORT ON MENTAL HEALTH

Social support plays a crucial role in our mental health. Humans are social creatures and contact with other people is of great importance for our well-being. Strong social support can help us reduce stress, regulate our emotions, and develop positive self-esteem.

THE DIFFERENT TYPES OF SOCIAL SUPPORT

There are different types of social support that can have a positive impact on our mental health. Emotional support involves feeling loved, accepted, and understood. It's about other people being there for us when we need them and supporting us in difficult times.

Instrumental support refers to practical help that helps us overcome challenges. These can be, for example, concrete actions such as help with household chores, childcare or coping with tasks.

Informational support involves sharing information, advice, and knowledge. When we are faced with problems, it can be helpful to get information and perspectives from other people to help us make better decisions.

THE BENEFITS OF SOCIAL SUPPORT

Social support can have a variety of benefits for our mental health. Strong social support can help reduce stress and reduce the risk of mental disorders. When we feel supported by other people, we often feel that we are not alone and that we can deal with our challenges.

Social support can also help regulate our emotions. When we can talk to other people about our feelings, we often feel relieved and can better understand and process our emotions.

In addition, social support can boost our self-esteem. When we are loved, accepted and appreciated by other people, we feel valuable and have a positive self-image. This can help us to better accept ourselves and love ourselves.

HOW TO BUILD SOCIAL SUPPORT

There are several ways to build and maintain social support. One way is to strengthen existing relationships. This means spending time with family and friends, sharing regularly and supporting each other.

It can also be helpful to make new social contacts. This can be done by participating in social activities, hobbies, or interest groups. By engaging in communities, we have the opportunity to meet people who have similar interests and experiences.

In addition, it may be useful to seek professional support. Therapists, counselors, or support groups can be a valuable source of support and help us improve our mental health.

THE IMPORTANCE OF MUTUAL SUPPORT

Social support is not a one-way street. It is important that we not only receive support from other people, but also that we are supportive ourselves. By helping and supporting other people, we can not only improve their mental health, but also increase our own well-being.

Mutual support can take various forms. It can mean that we are there for other people when they need us, listening to them and supporting them. It can also mean that we offer practical help or give them information and advice.

By supporting each other, we can build a strong community where everyone feels safe and supported. This can help reduce the stigma associated with mental illness and create an environment where people can talk openly about their mental health.

RESULT

Social support plays a crucial role in our mental health. Strong social support can help us reduce stress, regulate our emotions, and develop positive self-esteem. It is important to strengthen existing relationships, make new social contacts and seek professional support. Mutual support is also of great importance to build a strong community and promote the well-being of all.

DEALING WITH CONFLICTS IN RELATIONSHIPS

Conflict is a natural part of interpersonal relationships. They can occur in different situations, whether in the family, at work or in partnership. Dealing with conflict is crucial for well-being and mental health. In this section, we will learn about different strategies and techniques for managing conflict in relationships.

UNDERSTANDING AND COMMUNICATING CONFLICTS

The first step in dealing with conflict is to understand and communicate it. Conflicts often arise due to different needs, expectations or opinions. It is important to reflect on one's own perspective and understand the perspective of the other. Open and honest communication is key to clarifying misunderstandings and finding solutions.

CONFLICTING CONSTRUCTIVE PASSWORD

Conflicts can be resolved destructively or constructively. A destructive solution often leads to further problems and can put a strain on the relationship. A constructive solution, on the other hand, makes it possible to find common solutions and strengthen the relationship. Here are some techniques that can help with constructive conflict resolution:

Willingness to compromise: Be willing to compromise and look for common solutions. It is important that both parties consider their needs and desires.

Active listening: Listen actively and try to understand the other person's perspective. If necessary, repeat what you have heard to make sure you have understood correctly.

Use "I" messages: Use "I messages" to express your feelings and needs instead of blaming or criticizing the other person. This makes communication more respectful and constructive.

Identify common goals: Find common goals or interests to focus on. This can help shift the focus away from the points of conflict and create a positive atmosphere.

EMOTIONAL INTELLIGENCE AND EMPATHY

Emotional intelligence and empathy play an important role in dealing with conflict. Emotional intelligence refers to the ability to recognize and regulate one's emotions, as well as to understand other people's emotions. Empathy allows us to put ourselves in the other person's shoes and understand their feelings. These skills can help you better understand conflicts and respond appropriately.

SEEING CONFLICTS AS AN OPPORTUNITY FOR PERSONAL DEVELOPMENT

Conflicts can also be seen as an opportunity for personal development. They offer the opportunity to reflect on and change one's own behavioral patterns. Conflict can help us improve our communication skills, better understand our own needs, and strengthen our relationships. By viewing conflict as a learning opportunity, we can grow personally and boost our mental health.

GET PROFESSIONAL SUPPORT

Sometimes conflicts can be so complex or stressful that it makes sense to seek professional support. A mediator or therapist can help improve communication, resolve conflicts, and strengthen the relationship. It's important to realize that there's no shame in seeking professional help, and that it can be an important step in promoting mental health.

Dealing with conflict in relationships takes time, patience, and practice. It is important to be aware that conflicts are normal and that there are different ways to resolve them constructively. By improving our communication skills, developing empathy, and seeing conflict as an opportunity for personal development, we can strengthen our relationships and boost our mental health.

EXERCISE AND NUTRITION FOR MENTAL HEALTH

THE EFFECTS OF EXERCISE ON MENTAL HEALTH

Exercise has a significant impact on mental health. It is well known that physical activity has positive effects on the body, but its benefits also extend to mental health. Regular exercise can help reduce stress, improve mood, and increase overall well-being.

THE ROLE OF EXERCISE IN STRESS MANAGEMENT

Stress is a pervasive part of modern life and can have a negative impact on mental health. Fortunately, exercise can be an effective way to manage stress. Physical activity releases endorphins, which act as natural stress reduction hormones. These hormones can help improve mood and promote a sense of relaxation. In addition, exercise can also help reduce the physical tension that often accompanies stress.

THE EFFECTS OF EXERCISE ON MOOD

Exercise can also have a direct impact on mood. Physical activity releases various chemical compounds in the brain, including serotonin, dopamine, and norepinephrine. These neurotransmitters are known to regulate mood and create a sense of well-being. People who exercise regularly often report an improved mood and a heightened sense of satisfaction.

THE IMPORTANCE OF EXERCISE FOR SLEEP QUALITY

Another important impact of exercise on mental health is its positive effect on sleep quality. Regular physical activity can help regulate the sleep-wake cycle and improve sleep quality. A good night's sleep is crucial for mental health, as lack of sleep has been linked to increased susceptibility to stress, anxiety and depression. Regular exercise allows the body to rest better and get a good night's sleep.

MOVEMENT AS A SOCIAL ACTIVITY

Exercise can also be considered a social activity that can have positive effects on mental health. Playing sports or physical activity together with other people can strengthen a sense of belonging and social cohesion. This can help reduce loneliness and social isolation, which are often associated with mental health issues. In addition, participating in group activities can also help increase self-esteem and increase confidence in one's abilities.

PRACTICAL TIPS FOR INTEGRATING EXERCISE INTO EVERYDAY LIFE

There are many ways to incorporate exercise into everyday life, even for people with a hectic lifestyle. Here are some practical tips to incorporate more physical activity into your daily routine:

Choose activities that you enjoy: Find a form of exercise that brings you joy, whether it's dancing, cycling, swimming, or yoga. If you enjoy the activity, you're more likely to stick with it.

Set realistic goals: Start slowly and gradually increase your physical activity. Set realistic goals that you can achieve and reward yourself when you achieve those goals.

Take every opportunity to exercise: take the stairs instead of the elevator, walk or bike to work, or take a walk during your lunch break. Every form of movement counts.

Find a training partner: Training with a partner can be motivating and help you achieve your goals. They can support each other and hold each other accountable.

Schedule set times for exercise: Make exercise a priority by scheduling set times for it in your daily routine. Treat it like an appointment and stick to it.

Vary your activities: To avoid boredom and maintain motivation, vary your activities. Try different sports or activities to add variety.

Incorporating exercise into everyday life can have a significant impact on mental health. It's important to remember that any form of exercise counts and that regular physical activity can provide long-term mental health benefits.

PRACTICAL TIPS FOR INTEGRATING EXERCISE INTO EVERYDAY LIFE

Exercise plays a crucial role in our mental health. Regular physical activity can help reduce stress, improve mood, and increase overall well-being. But we often find it difficult to integrate enough exercise into our everyday lives. In this section, we will discuss practical tips for incorporating exercise into everyday life.

FIND ACTIVITIES YOU ENJOY

The first step to incorporating exercise into your daily routine is to find activities that you enjoy. If you enjoy a particular activity, you will be more motivated to do it regularly. Think about what forms of exercise you might like. You may be interested in dancing, yoga, swimming, or cycling. Try different activities and see which one you like best.

PLAN EXERCISE INTO YOUR DAILY ROUTINE

In order to integrate exercise into everyday life, it is important to plan it into your daily routine. Set specific goals and set fixed times when you want to move. Consider whether you can find time for exercise in the morning before work, during your lunch break, or in the evening after work. By making exercise a permanent habit, it will be easier for you to incorporate it into your daily routine.

USE ACTIVE MEANS OF TRANSPORT

An easy way to get more exercise into your daily routine is to use active means of transportation. For example, instead of taking the car, you could walk or cycle more often. If possible, you could also use public transport and walk part of the way. These small changes can help bring more movement into your everyday life.

TAKE BREAKS FROM MOVEMENT

If you have a sedentary job, it is important to take regular breaks from exercise. Get up every 30 minutes and do some simple exercises to mobilize your body. For example, you could do stretching exercises for a few minutes or take a short walk around the office building. These short breaks in movement can help relieve tension and improve blood circulation.

CONNECTING MOVEMENT WITH OTHERS

Connecting exercise with others can provide extra motivation. For example, meet up regularly with friends to do sports together or join a sports group. The social component makes exercise a pleasant and entertaining experience. In addition, you can motivate and support each other to be active on a regular basis.

CONSCIOUS USE OF EVERYDAY ACTIVITIES

Make conscious use of everyday activities to bring more movement into your everyday life. Instead of taking the elevator, you could take the stairs. When shopping, you could consciously take further paths instead of choosing the shortest route. Small changes like these can help incorporate more exercise into your daily routine without having to invest extra time.

LEVERAGING TECHNOLOGY

Use modern technology to incorporate exercise into your daily routine. There are numerous fitness apps and wearables that can help you monitor your movement and stay motivated. For example, you can use a pedometer to make sure you're taking enough steps a day. Or you could use a fitness app that offers you different exercises and workout plans.

REWARDING YOURSELF

Reward yourself when you reach your exercise goals. Set yourself small milestones and reward yourself, for example, with a relaxing bath, a trip to the cinema or a delicious meal if you have been active on a regular basis. These rewards can help maintain your motivation and help you incorporate exercise into your daily routine in the long term.

FLEXIBILITY AND REALISM

Be flexible and realistic about your movement goals. It is not always possible to exercise intensively every day. Accept that sometimes there are days when you have less time or energy for exercise. Set realistic goals that you can achieve and, if necessary, adapt them to your current life circumstances.

Incorporating exercise into everyday life takes time and commitment, but the benefits to your mental health are worth it. By being active on a regular basis, you can reduce stress, improve your mood, and increase your overall well-being. Try the tips above and find out which strategies suit you best.

THE IMPORTANCE OF A BALANCED DIET FOR MENTAL HEALTH

A balanced diet plays a crucial role in our physical health, but it also has a significant impact on our mental health. The food we eat can affect our mood, energy levels, and mental performance. A poor diet can lead to a deterioration in mental health, while a healthy diet can help improve it.

THE EFFECTS OF NUTRIENT DEFICIENCIES ON MENTAL HEALTH

A lack of certain nutrients can lead to a number of mental health problems. For example, a lack of omega-3 fatty acids, which are mainly found in fish and nuts, may be associated with increased susceptibility to depression and anxiety. Omega-3 fatty acids are important for brain function and can reduce inflammation in the body that has been linked to mental illness.

Another important nutrient for mental health is vitamin D. It is mainly produced by sun exposure to the skin, but can also be ingested through certain foods such as fish, eggs, and mushrooms. Vitamin D deficiency has been linked to an increased risk of depression and mood disorders. Vitamin D is believed to affect the production of serotonin, a neurotransmitter responsible for regulating mood.

In addition, a lack of B vitamins, especially vitamin B12 and folic acid, can lead to a deterioration in mental health. These vitamins are important for the production of neurotransmitters, which are responsible for communication between nerve cells in the brain. A deficiency of these vitamins can lead to symptoms such as fatigue, irritability, memory problems, and depression.

THE ROLE OF ANTIOXIDANTS IN MENTAL HEALTH

Antioxidants are compounds that can protect the body from free radical damage. Free radicals are unstable molecules that can be produced in the body by various factors such as pollution, smoking, and stress. High levels of free radicals in the body can lead to oxidative stress, which has been linked to a number of mental illnesses such as depression, anxiety and dementia.

A diet rich in antioxidants can help reduce oxidative stress and improve mental health. Foods such as berries, green leafy vegetables, nuts, and dark chocolate are rich in antioxidants and can help support brain function and improve mood.

THE IMPORTANCE OF STABLE BLOOD SUGAR LEVELS FOR MENTAL HEALTH

Stable blood sugar levels are important for maintaining a stable mood and energy. When blood sugar levels fluctuate greatly, it can lead to mood swings, irritability, and lack of energy. A diet rich in refined carbohydrates and sugar can lead to rapid spikes and drops in blood sugar, which can have a negative impact on mental health.

It is therefore important to have a balanced diet rich in carbohydrates rich in fiber, such as whole grains, fruits and vegetables. These foods are digested more slowly and help keep blood sugar levels stable. In addition, eating protein-rich foods such as lean meats, fish, legumes, and nuts can help stabilize blood sugar levels and maintain energy throughout the day.

THE ROLE OF GUT HEALTH IN MENTAL HEALTH

The health of our gut has a significant impact on our mental health. The gut is connected to the brain via the so-called gut-brain axis, through which signals are exchanged between the gut and the brain. A disturbed intestinal flora, also known as dysbiosis, can lead to inflammation in the body and increase the risk of mental illness.

A diet rich in fiber and probiotic foods can help improve gut health and promote mental health. Fiber is food for the good bacteria in the gut and helps maintain a healthy gut flora. Probiotic foods such as yogurt, sauerkraut, and kefir contain live bacterial cultures that can support gut health.

PRACTICAL TIPS FOR A BALANCED DIET

Make sure you eat a varied diet that contains all the important nutrients.

Eat meals regularly and avoid long meal breaks.

Choose whole grains instead of refined carbohydrates.

Eat an adequate amount of fruits and vegetables.

Avoid excessive consumption of sugary foods and drinks.

Drink plenty of water to stay hydrated.

Consider the consumption of omega-3 fatty acids by eating fish, nuts and seeds.

Make sure you get enough vitamin D from sun exposure and eating certain foods.

Get enough B vitamins by eating meat, fish, eggs, and green leafy vegetables.

Add foods rich in antioxidants to your diet, such as berries, green leafy vegetables, and nuts.

Avoid excessive consumption of alcohol and caffeine as they can have a negative impact on mental health.

A balanced diet is an important part of mental health. By paying attention to our diet and developing healthy eating habits, we can help improve our mood, energy levels, and mental performance.

DEVELOPING HEALTHY EATING HABITS

A healthy diet plays a crucial role in our mental health. The foods we eat can have a direct impact on our mood, energy levels, and mental performance. By developing healthy eating habits, we can improve our mental health and achieve better well-being in the long term.

THE IMPORTANCE OF A BALANCED DIET

A balanced diet is the key to good mental health. It provides our body with the necessary nutrients to function optimally. A balanced diet consists of a variety of foods that contain all the essential nutrients, such as fruits, vegetables, whole grains, lean meats, fish, legumes, and healthy fats.

A balanced diet helps keep blood sugar levels stable, which in turn has an impact on our mood and energy levels. If we regularly eat unhealthy foods that are high in sugar and saturated fat, it can lead to mood swings, lack of energy, and increased susceptibility to mental illness.

PRACTICAL TIPS FOR DEVELOPING HEALTHY EATING HABITS

To develop healthy eating habits, it is important to make small but sustainable changes in our diet. Here are some practical tips that can help you:

Plan your meals in advance: By planning your meals in advance, you can ensure that you are eating balanced and healthy meals. Take the time to make a weekly schedule and make a shopping list to make sure you have all the necessary ingredients on hand.

Eat regularly: Don't skip meals and try to eat regularly. This helps to keep blood sugar levels stable and avoid energy holes.

Add more fruits and vegetables: Fruits and vegetables are rich in vitamins, minerals, and fiber, which are important for good mental health. Try to add a serving of fruits or vegetables at each meal.

Choose whole grains: Whole grains such as whole wheat bread, whole wheat pasta, and brown rice contain more fiber and nutrients than refined grain products. They help to keep blood sugar levels stable and provide long-lasting energy.

Reduce your consumption of sugary drinks: Sugary drinks such as soda and sweetened juices contain a lot of empty calories and can lead to mood swings and lack of energy. Instead, drink water, unsweetened tea, or diluted fruit juices.

Cook for yourself: By cooking yourself, you have control over the ingredients and can ensure that your meals are healthy and balanced. Experiment with new recipes and try different foods to diversify your diet.

Pay attention to portion sizes: It's important to follow the right portion sizes to avoid overeating. Read the nutritional information on the packaging and use measuring cups to measure the right amount of food.

THE EFFECTS OF UNHEALTHY DIET ON MENTAL HEALTH

An unhealthy diet can have a negative impact on our mental health. Regular consumption of unhealthy foods rich in sugar, saturated fat, and trans fats can lead to an increased inflammatory response in the body. This inflammation can increase the risk of mental health conditions such as depression and anxiety.

In addition, an unhealthy diet can lead to an imbalance in the intestinal flora. A healthy gut flora is important for the production of neurotransmitters such as serotonin, which is important for our mood and well-being. If the intestinal flora is disturbed, it can lead to mood problems and increased susceptibility to mental illness.

THE IMPORTANCE OF NUTRIENTS FOR MENTAL HEALTH

Certain nutrients play an important role in our mental health. Here are some key nutrients and their effects on mental health:

Omega-3 fatty acids: Omega-3 fatty acids are essential fatty acids that are important for healthy brain function. They can help reduce inflammation and reduce the risk of depression and anxiety. Good sources of omega-3 fatty acids include fish, flaxseed, and walnuts.

B vitamins: B vitamins, especially vitamin B12 and folic acid, are important for the production of neurotransmitters and the maintenance of healthy brain function. They can help alleviate mood problems and reduce the risk of depression. Good sources of B vitamins include whole grains, legumes, and green leafy vegetables.

Antioxidants: Antioxidants such as vitamin C and vitamin E can help reduce oxidative stress in the brain and reduce the risk of neurodegenerative diseases. Good sources of antioxidants include fruits, vegetables, and nuts.

Magnesium: Magnesium is a mineral that is important for healthy brain function. It can help reduce stress and improve mood. Good sources of magnesium include whole grains, nuts, and green leafy vegetables.

By eating a balanced diet and getting enough of these nutrients, we can support our mental health and improve our well-being.

RESULT

Developing healthy eating habits is an important step in boosting our mental health. A balanced diet provides our body with the necessary nutrients to function optimally and can help reduce mood problems and reduce the risk of mental illness. By following practical tips on how to incorporate healthy eating habits into our daily lives, we can achieve better well-being in the long run.

RELAXATION TECHNIQUES AND STRESS RELIEF

THE IMPORTANCE OF RELAXATION FOR MENTAL HEALTH

Relaxation plays a crucial role in mental health. In our hectic and stressful world, it's important to schedule regular time for relaxation and recuperation. Through relaxation techniques, we can calm our minds, reduce stress, and improve our emotional well-being.

THE EFFECTS OF STRESS ON MENTAL HEALTH

Stress is a natural part of life and can even be helpful in certain situations. However, when we are exposed to chronic stress, it can have a negative impact on our mental health. Long-term stress can lead to anxiety, depression, sleep disorders, and other mental disorders.

Stress also affects our physical health by weakening the immune system and increasing the risk of heart disease, diabetes, and other chronic conditions. Therefore, it is important to recognize stress in time and learn effective stress management techniques.

THE DIFFERENT RELAXATION TECHNIQUES

There are several relaxation techniques that can help us reduce stress and improve our mental health. Every person is unique, so it is important to find the technique that suits us best. Here are some of the most popular relaxation techniques:

Progressive muscle relaxation

Progressive muscle relaxation is a technique in which we contract different muscle groups one by one and then relax. Through this method, we can learn to consciously perceive the tension in our muscles and release it in a targeted manner. This leads to deep physical and mental relaxation.

Breathing

Breathing exercises are a simple and effective way to reduce stress and calm the mind. Through conscious breathing, we can oxygenate our body and focus on the present moment. There are different breathing techniques, such as abdominal breathing or the 4-7-8 method, that can help us relax and reduce stress.

Meditation

Meditation is a centuries-old practice that helps us calm our minds and find inner peace. Through regular meditation, we can learn to observe our thoughts and emotions without getting carried away by them. This allows us to achieve a clear and calm state of mind and reduce stress.

Yoga

Yoga is a holistic practice that connects body, mind and soul. By combining physical exercises, breathing techniques and meditation, we can strengthen our bodies, improve flexibility and reduce stress. Yoga also helps us focus on the present moment and quiet our thoughts.

PRACTICAL TIPS FOR COPING WITH STRESS IN EVERYDAY LIFE

In order to benefit from the positive effects of relaxation on mental health, it is important to regularly incorporate relaxation techniques into our daily lives. Here are some practical tips for managing stress:

Schedule regular relaxation times into your daily routine. Consciously take time for relaxation and recuperation.

Find the relaxation technique that suits you best. Try different techniques and choose the one that suits you the most.

Create a relaxing environment. Design your living space or workplace in such a way that it offers you peace and relaxation.

Take regular breaks. Treat yourself to short breaks to calm your mind and recharge your batteries.

Maintain social contacts. Spend time with your loved ones and share your feelings. Social support can be a great help in coping with stress.

Maintain a healthy lifestyle. A balanced diet, regular physical activity, and adequate sleep also contribute to mental health.

THE IMPACT OF RELAXATION ON MENTAL HEALTH

Relaxation has a positive impact on mental health. By relaxing regularly, we can reduce stress, calm our thoughts, and better regulate our emotions. This leads to improved emotional well-being and an increased quality of life.

In addition, relaxation can also relieve physical discomfort, lower blood pressure and strengthen the immune system. By making time for relaxation on a regular basis, we invest in our mental and physical health.

Overall, relaxation is an important part of mental health. By consciously taking time for relaxation and recuperation and learning effective relaxation techniques, we can reduce our stress and improve our mental health.

GET TO KNOW DIFFERENT RELAXATION TECHNIQUES

Relaxation techniques are an important way to reduce stress and promote mental health. There are several techniques that can help you relax your body and mind and find inner peace. In this section, we will learn about some of these techniques and how they can be used to reduce stress and increase well-being.

PROGRESSIVE MUSCLE RELAXATION

Progressive muscle relaxation is a technique in which the muscles are tensed one by one and then relaxed. By consciously tensing and relaxing the muscles, a deep relaxation of the entire body is achieved. This technique can help relieve muscle tension and reduce stress. To perform progressive muscle relaxation, you can sit or lie down in a quiet place and begin to tense your muscles one by one and then relax. For example, start with your feet and slowly work your way up through the body.

BREATHING

Breathing exercises are a simple and effective way to reduce stress and calm the mind. Through conscious breathing, you can focus your attention on the present moment and achieve deep relaxation. A simple breathing exercise is to inhale slowly and deeply through your nose and then slowly exhale through your mouth. As you exhale, you can imagine yourself letting go of stress and tension. Repeat this exercise several times, concentrating completely on your breath.

MEDITATION

Meditation is a technique that has been used for centuries to relax and promote well-being. Through meditation, you can calm your mind and find inner peace. There are different types of meditation, but a simple method is to sit or lie down in a quiet place and focus on your breath or a specific mantra. Let your thoughts pass without giving them meaning, and keep coming back to your breath or mantra focus.

YOGA

Yoga is a holistic practice that connects body, mind and soul. It combines physical exercises, breathing techniques, and meditation to reduce stress and promote mental health. Through the different yoga poses (asanas), you can stretch and strengthen your body while calming your mind. Yoga can also help improve flexibility and correct posture. There are different types of yoga, from gentle and relaxing practices to more sophisticated and powerful styles.

AUTOGENES TRAINING

Autogenic training is a relaxation technique in which you focus on specific formulas or phrases to achieve deep relaxation. These formulas are repeated internally and help to put the body and mind in a relaxed state. Autogenic training can help reduce stress, reduce anxiety and increase overall well-being. To perform autogenic training, you can sit or lie down in a quiet place and focus on a formula such as "I am calm and relaxed". Repeat this formula several times, letting go of all tension.

MASSAGE

Massage is a physical technique that can be not only relaxing but also beneficial for mental health. Through gentle touches and targeted pressure on certain areas of the body, muscle tension can be released and the body can be put into a state of relaxation. Massage can also help calm the mind and reduce stress. There are different types of massage techniques, from classic Swedish massage to aromatherapy massage with essential oils.

These different relaxation techniques can help you reduce stress, promote mental health, and increase overall well-being. It's important to set aside time for relaxation and self-care on a regular basis, and to find the techniques that suit you best. Experiment with different techniques and find out which ones will help you the most to relax and find inner peace.

PRACTICAL TIPS FOR COPING WITH STRESS IN EVERYDAY LIFE

Stress is a pervasive part of our modern lives. Whether it's the demands of the workplace, financial stresses, relationship problems, or other challenges, stress can have a negative impact on our mental health. Luckily, however, there are several practical tips and techniques that can help you better manage stress in everyday life and boost your mental health.

TIME MANAGEMENT

One of the most important strategies for managing stress is effective time management. By organizing and prioritizing your time well, you can avoid feeling overwhelmed by too many tasks. Here are some practical tips for effective time management:

Make a to-do list: write down all the tasks that need to be done and prioritize them according to their urgency. Start with the most important tasks and then work your way down.

Set realistic goals: Be honest with yourself and set realistic goals. Don't overload yourself with too many tasks, but focus on the essentials.

Delegate tasks: If possible, delegate tasks to other people. You don't have to do everything on your own.

Schedule breaks: Take regular short breaks to recover and recharge your batteries. This can help you be more productive and reduce stress.

RELAXATION

Relaxation techniques are an effective way to reduce stress and promote mental health. Here are some practical tips on how to incorporate relaxation into your daily routine:

Deep breathing: Take regular time to breathe in and out deeply. Focus on your breath and let go of all thoughts. This can help you calm down and reduce stress.

Progressive muscle relaxation: Tense different muscle groups one at a time and then relax them again. For example, start with the shoulders and work your way up to the toes. This technique can help relieve physical tension and promote relaxation.

Meditation: Find a quiet place, sit comfortably, and focus on your breath or a calming mantra. Meditation can help you calm the mind and reduce stress.

Yoga: Practice yoga regularly to relax your body and mind. Yoga combines physical exercises with breathing techniques and meditation and can help you reduce stress and promote mental health.

SELF-CARE

Self-care is an important aspect of managing stress and promoting mental health. Here are some practical tips on how to take better care of yourself:

Prioritize your needs: Take time for yourself and do things that bring you joy. Put your own needs first and take regular time off.

Maintain healthy habits: Make sure you eat a balanced diet, get enough sleep, and get regular physical activity. These factors can have a positive impact on your mental health and reduce stress.

Seek social support: Talk to friends, family, or a therapist about your worries and fears. Sharing with others can help you reduce stress and gain new perspectives.

Do things that bring you joy: Make time for hobbies and activities that you enjoy. This can help you reduce stress and promote positive emotions.

MINDFULNESS IN EVERYDAY LIFE

Mindfulness is a technique that can help you become aware of the present moment and reduce stress. Here are some practical tips on how to incorporate mindfulness into your daily routine:

Take conscious time-outs: Sit down regularly and concentrate on your sensory perceptions. Be aware of what you see, hear, smell, taste and feel.

Eat mindfully: Take time to eat consciously and enjoy every bite. Focus on the taste, texture, and smell of the food.

Be present in the moment: Try not to let your mind wander to the past or future, but focus on the present moment. This can help you reduce stress and boost your mental health.

Practice mindful movement: When you play sports or engage in physical activity, be aware of your movements and feel how your body feels.

By incorporating these practical stress management tips into your daily routine, you can strengthen your mental health and live a more balanced life. Experiment with different techniques and see what works best for you. Remember that managing stress is an individual process and it is important to pay attention to your own needs.

THE IMPACT OF RELAXATION ON MENTAL HEALTH

Relaxation plays a crucial role in our mental health. In our hectic and stressful world, it's important to schedule regular time for relaxation and recuperation. Through relaxation techniques, we can calm our minds, reduce stress, and improve our emotional well-being.

THE IMPORTANCE OF RELAXATION

Relaxation is an important part of a healthy lifestyle. It allows us to regenerate our body and mind and recharge our batteries. Through relaxation, we can reduce stress, clear our thoughts, and balance our emotions. It helps us to recover from the stresses of everyday life and to strengthen our mental health.

GET TO KNOW DIFFERENT RELAXATION TECHNIQUES

There are several relaxation techniques that can help us calm down and calm our minds. Here are some popular techniques:

Progressive muscle relaxation

Progressive muscle relaxation is a method in which we tense and relax different muscle groups one after the other. Through this technique, we can release tension in our body and relax deeply.

Breathing

Breathing exercises are a simple and effective way to reduce stress and calm our minds. Through conscious breathing, we can oxygenate our body and focus on the present moment.

Meditation

Meditation is an ancient practice where we quiet our minds and focus on the present moment. Through regular meditation, we can observe and let go of our thoughts, reduce stress, and improve our emotional well-being.

Yoga

Yoga is a holistic practice that connects body, mind and soul. Through yoga exercises, we can stretch and strengthen our bodies, calm our minds, and control our breathing. Yoga helps us reduce stress and boost our mental health.

PRACTICAL TIPS FOR COPING WITH STRESS IN EVERYDAY LIFE

To integrate relaxation into our daily life and reduce stress, we can follow these tips:

Schedule regular time for relaxation. Take conscious breaks and treat yourself to moments of rest and relaxation.

Find a relaxation technique that suits you best. Try different techniques and choose the one that suits you the most.

Create a relaxing environment. Design your living space or workplace in such a way that it gives you a feeling of calm and relaxation.

Take time for yourself. Do things that bring you joy and help you relax, such as taking a warm bath, reading a book, or going for a walk.

Make sure you have a good work-life balance. Find a balance between work and leisure and make time for hobbies and social activities on a regular basis.

Practice mindfulness. Be present in the present moment and be aware of your thoughts and feelings without judging or judging them.

THE IMPACT OF RELAXATION ON MENTAL HEALTH

Relaxation has a positive impact on our mental health. By making time for relaxation on a regular basis, we can reduce stress, calm our minds, and balance our emotions. Relaxation helps us strengthen our mental health and prevent mental disorders.

Stress is a common trigger for mental disorders such as anxiety disorders and depression. By relaxing, we can reduce stress and increase our resilience to stressful situations. Relaxation techniques such as meditation and yoga can help us calm our minds and let go of negative emotions.

In addition, relaxation can also improve our sleep quality. A good night's sleep is important for our mental health because it helps us reduce stress and regulate our emotions. Through relaxation, we can calm our minds and promote better sleep.

Overall, relaxation is an important part of a healthy lifestyle and plays a crucial role in our mental health. By making time for relaxation on a regular basis and practicing various relaxation techniques, we can reduce stress, calm our minds, and improve our emotional well-being.

PREVENTION AND LONG-TERM MENTAL HEALTH

THE IMPORTANCE OF PREVENTION FOR MENTAL HEALTH

Mental health is a valuable asset that needs to be protected and preserved. Prevention plays a crucial role in this. It includes measures aimed at preventing mental disorders before they even occur. Prevention is an important part of health care and can help improve people's well-being and quality of life.

PRIMARY PREVENTION

Primary prevention aims to prevent mental disorders in the first place. It focuses on promoting mental health and protecting against risk factors. An important aspect of primary prevention is mental health education and raising people's awareness of the importance of mental health. Targeted information campaigns can reduce prejudice and stigmatisation.

In addition, primary prevention also includes measures to promote a healthy lifestyle. Regular physical activity, a balanced diet, and getting enough sleep are important factors that can contribute to mental health. By imparting knowledge and providing resources, people can be encouraged to incorporate healthy habits into their daily lives.

SECONDARY PREVENTION

Secondary prevention aims to detect and treat mental disorders at an early stage. It focuses on early detection of symptoms and timely intervention to prevent or slow the progression of the disorder. Early intervention can help people get faster access to appropriate treatment and improve their chances of recovery.

An important part of secondary prevention is regular mental health monitoring. Through screening programs and questionnaires, potential signs of mental disorders can be detected. This makes it possible to take appropriate measures at an early stage and refer those affected to the right professionals.

TERTIÄRE PRÄVENTION

Tertiary prevention aims to support people with pre-existing mental disorders and improve their quality of life. It focuses on rehabilitation and the promotion of long-term mental health. Tertiary prevention includes measures such as therapy, medication and social support to help sufferers cope with their disorder and enable them to live a fulfilling life.

An important aspect of tertiary prevention is the promotion of self-help. By teaching coping strategies and strengthening self-efficacy, people can learn to manage their disorder and improve their quality of life. Support groups and peer counseling can also be a valuable resource to support people with mental health disorders and give them a sense of community.

THE ROLE OF SOCIETY

Promoting mental health is a task that affects society as a whole. A supportive and inclusive society can help prevent mental disorders and provide adequate support to those affected. It's important to break down prejudice and stigma and encourage an open discussion about mental health.

Creating a healthy work environment is also of great importance. Employers can take steps to reduce workplace stress and promote employee mental health. This can be done, for example, through flexible working hours, regular breaks, and access to support programs.

In addition, it is important that the health system allocates adequate resources for mental health. Access to qualified professionals and appropriate treatment is crucial to support people with mental health disorders. Investing in mental health can lead to a reduction in the burden of disease and an improvement in quality of life in the long term.

Overall, prevention is an important approach to promote mental health and prevent mental disorders. Through targeted action at the individual, societal and political levels, we can help ensure that mental health is recognised as an integral part of well-being and quality of life.

EARLY DETECTION OF MENTAL DISORDERS

Early detection of mental disorders plays a crucial role in maintaining mental health. By recognizing signs and symptoms of mental disorders early, we can act in time and seek appropriate support and treatment. In this section, we will look at the different aspects of early detection of mental disorders and how we can implement them effectively.

THE IMPORTANCE OF EARLY DETECTION

Early detection of mental disorders is of great importance, as it allows us to take timely measures to prevent or slow down the progression of the disorder. Often, mental disorders are not recognized until they are already advanced and have a significant impact on a person's life. However, by detecting it early, we can reduce the likelihood of complications and increase the chances of successful treatment.

SIGNS AND SYMPTOMS OF MENTAL DISORDERS

There are various signs and symptoms that can indicate the presence of a mental disorder. These can vary from person to person and depend on the type of disorder. Some common signs and symptoms may include:
Changes in sleep patterns, such as insomnia or excessive sleep
Mood swings, such as persistent sadness, irritability, or anxiety
Loss of interest in activities that used to be enjoyable
Difficulty concentrating or making decisions

Changes in eating behaviors, such as overeating or loss of appetite

Withdrawal from social activities and isolation

Physical ailments without an identifiable medical cause, such as headaches or stomach problems

It is important to note that the presence of these signs and symptoms does not necessarily indicate the presence of a mental disorder. However, it is advisable to seek professional help if symptoms persist or worsen.

SCREENING PROCEDURE

In order to detect mental disorders at an early stage, various screening procedures are used. These procedures are used to identify potential signs and symptoms and to make an initial assessment. A commonly used screening procedure is the Mental Disorders Questionnaire (EPDS), which is specifically aimed at detecting depression. There are also other screening procedures that target specific disorders such as anxiety disorders or eating disorders.

These screening procedures can be performed by healthcare professionals, psychologists, or therapists. They consist of a series of questions that aim to gather information about a person's emotional well-being, behavior, and thought patterns. Based on the answers, a preliminary assessment can be made as to whether a mental disorder could be present.

WHEN SHOULD YOU SEEK PROFESSIONAL HELP?

It is important to know when to seek professional help in order to get proper diagnosis and treatment. If you have persistent or worsening symptoms that interfere with your daily life or cause you concern, you should consult a professional. This can be a psychiatrist, psychologist, or therapist who specializes in mental health.

In addition, you should seek professional help if you have suicidal thoughts or feel that you may be harming yourself or others. In such cases, it is important to get immediate support to ensure your safety.

THE ROLE OF THE COMMUNITY IN EARLY DETECTION

The community plays an important role in the early detection of mental disorders. Through education and awareness, we can promote mental health awareness and encourage people to seek professional help when they need it. Schools, workplaces, and community organizations can provide programs and resources to support early detection of mental disorders.

In addition, it is important to create a supportive and stigma-free environment where people can talk openly about their mental health without fear of prejudice or discrimination. By tackling the stigma of mental disorders, we can encourage people to seek help early and boost their mental health.

RESULT

Early detection of mental disorders is crucial to get timely support and treatment. By paying attention to signs and symptoms, using screening procedures, and seeking professional help, we can prevent or slow the progression of mental disorders. The community plays an important role in promoting early detection and creating a supportive environment for people with mental disorders. It is important to promote mental health awareness and combat stigma to promote long-term mental health.

MEASURES TO PROMOTE LONG-TERM MENTAL HEALTH

Promoting long-term mental health is vital to living a full and happy life. There are several steps that everyone can take to support and strengthen their mental health in the long term. In this section, we'll take a closer look at some of these measures.

MAINTAINING A HEALTHY LIFESTYLE

A healthy lifestyle is an important factor in long-term mental health. This includes a balanced diet, regular physical activity and sufficient sleep. A balanced diet rich in fruits, vegetables, whole grains, and lean protein can help improve mood and increase energy levels. Regular physical activity, such as walking, jogging or yoga, can reduce stress and increase overall well-being. Getting enough sleep is also important to promote mental health. It is recommended to get at least seven to nine hours of sleep per night.

LEARN STRESS MANAGEMENT TECHNIQUES

Stress is a natural part of life, but chronic stress can have a negative impact on mental health. Therefore, it is important to learn and apply effective stress management techniques. These include relaxation techniques such as meditation, breathing exercises, and progressive muscle relaxation. These techniques can help reduce stress, promote relaxation, and improve overall well-being. It is also important to take time for yourself and find activities that bring joy and reduce stress, such as hobbies, reading or listening to music.

SEEKING SOCIAL SUPPORT

Social support is another important factor in long-term mental health. It's important to build and maintain relationships, whether it's with family, friends, or other trusted people. These relationships can serve as a support system, helping to reduce stress, manage problems, and improve overall well-being. It's also important to get involved in social activities and connect with other people, whether it's through volunteer work, hobbies, or community events.

PRACTICING MINDFULNESS

Mindfulness is a technique that can help raise awareness of the present moment and reduce stress. Through mindfulness exercises such as meditation, yoga or conscious breathing, one can learn to let go of negative thoughts and focus on the here and now. Mindfulness can also help build self-acceptance and self-esteem by becoming aware that you don't have to be perfect and that it's important to treat yourself with kindness and compassion.

SETTING BOUNDARIES AND PRACTICING SELF-CARE

It's important to set boundaries and protect yourself to promote long-term mental health. This means saying "no" when you're overloaded and making time for rest and recuperation. Self-care also involves paying attention to one's needs and treating oneself with kindness and compassion. This can mean taking regular breaks, indulging in things that bring you joy, and making time for self-reflection and personal growth.

SEEK PROFESSIONAL HELP

If you feel that your efforts to promote mental health are not enough, or if you are facing more severe mental health issues, it is important to seek professional help. A psychologist or psychiatrist can assist in the diagnosis and treatment of mental disorders and recommend appropriate treatment options. It's important to understand that there's no shame in seeking professional help, and that it can be an important step in promoting long-term mental health.

Promoting long-term mental health requires continuous effort and dedication. By maintaining a healthy lifestyle, learning stress management techniques, seeking social support, practicing mindfulness, setting boundaries, and practicing self-care, one can support one's mental health in the long term and live a full and happy life. It is also important to seek professional help if necessary to get the best possible support.

THE ROLE OF SOCIETY IN SUPPORTING MENTAL HEALTH

Mental health is an important issue that not only has an impact on individuals, but is also influenced by society as a whole. The role of society in supporting mental health cannot be underestimated, as it has a direct impact on people's well-being and quality of life.

AWARENESS-RAISING AND EDUCATION

One of the most important tasks of society is to raise awareness of mental health and educate people about the different aspects of mental disorders. Targeted awareness campaigns and information events can reduce prejudice and stigmatisation. It is important that society takes mental health as seriously as physical health and that people with mental disorders are not discriminated against or marginalised.

ACCESS TO ADEQUATE CARE

Society has a responsibility to ensure that people with mental disorders have access to adequate care. This includes access to qualified professionals such as psychologists and psychiatrists, but also to support services such as counselling centres and support groups. It is important that these services are accessible to all people, regardless of their social or economic background.

CREATING A SUPPORTIVE ENVIRONMENT

Society can create a supportive environment that helps people with mental disorders recover and live fulfilling lives. This can be done by creating inclusive communities and workplaces where people with mental health disorders are accepted and supported. It is important that society breaks down barriers and provides people with mental disorders with the same opportunities and opportunities as everyone else.

PROMOTION OF SOCIAL SUPPORT

Social support plays a crucial role in mental health. Society can help to strengthen and promote social support systems. This can be done by creating networks and community organizations that help people with mental disorders socialize and receive support. It is important that people with mental disorders are not isolated, but integrated into the community.

PREVENTION AND EARLY DETECTION

Society can play an important role in the prevention of mental disorders by identifying risk factors and taking steps to reduce them. This can be done by promoting a healthy lifestyle, reducing stressors, and creating a supportive environment. In addition, early detection of mental disorders is crucial to enable timely treatment. Society can help raise awareness of the signs and symptoms of mental disorders and facilitate access to diagnostic services.

POLICY SUPPORT AND RESOURCES

Society can provide policy support and resources to promote mental health. This includes providing sufficient funding for mental health care, developing policies and programs to promote mental health, and collaborating with other relevant organizations and institutions. It is important that mental health is highly valued in society and that the necessary resources are allocated to meet people's needs.

The role of society in supporting mental health is crucial. By raising awareness, improving access to care, creating a supportive environment, fostering social support, enabling prevention and early detection, and providing policy support and resources, society can help improve people's mental health and promote the well-being of society as a whole.